I Am Indeed Your Brother

I Am Indeed Your Brother

A Servant of Jesus among Allah's Poor

Bob McCahill

ORBIS BOOKS
Maryknoll, New York 10545

ORBIS BOOKS
Maryknoll, New York 10545

Fathers and Brothers
MARYKNOLL™

Founded in 1970, Orbis Books endeavors to publish works that enlighten the mind, nourish the spirit, and challenge the conscience. The publishing arm of the Maryknoll Fathers and Brothers, Orbis seeks to explore the global dimensions of the Christian faith and mission, to invite dialogue with diverse cultures and religious traditions, and to serve the cause of reconciliation and peace. The books published reflect the views of their authors and do not represent the official position of the Maryknoll Society. To learn more about Maryknoll and Orbis Books, please visit our website at www.maryknollsociety.org.

The publisher acknowledges with thanks the work of Victor Edwin, SJ, Director of the Vidyajyoti Institute of Islamic Studies in Delhi, India, who first proposed this volume and worked with the author to bring it to fruition.

Manufactured in the United States of America

Library of Congress Cataloging-in-Publication Data

Names: McCahill, Bob, author.
Title: I am indeed your brother : a servant of Jesus among Allah's poor / Bob McCahill.
Description: Maryknoll, NY : Orbis Books, [2018]
Identifiers: LCCN 2018016952 (print) | LCCN 2018032398 (ebook) | ISBN 9781608337620 (e-book) | ISBN 9781626982963 (pbk) | ISBN 9781608337620 (ebook)
Subjects: LCSH: McCahill, Bob. | Missionaries—Bangladesh--Biography. | Missionaries—United States—Biography. | Missions to Muslims—Bangladesh.
Classification: LCC BV2626.M38 (ebook) | LCC BV2626.M38 A3 2018 (print) | DDC 266/.2092 [B]—dc23
LC record available at https://lccn.loc.gov/2018016952

*This book is dedicated to
the Rohingya refugees
who endure immense sufferings
and
who inspire the rest of us
to face hardships
without complaining*

Contents

Contents

Foreword

October 31st is the date that Bob McCahill first realized that he was being called by God. He heard that call; his response led him to the Maryknoll Mission Society and a lifetime dedicated to being in mission in another country and culture, among the poor. Every October 31st Fr. Bob McCahill writes to friends, family, and benefactors celebrating his first awareness of God's call and sharing highlights of his experiences in mission. This book, the compiled letters of a life in mission, gives clear and vivid images of what evangelization and mission are all about today. The illustration of evangelization painted by Fr. Bob is vibrant and down to earth. He is a great storyteller. With each letter and each story Fr. Bob reveals different elements of his mission theology and components of his faith journey. They are interwoven to reveal a life of service, witness, and joy—a life lived for others. The resulting personal fulfillment and joy are a clear reflection of the joy pointed to by Pope Francis in *The Joy of the Gospel*.

Pope Francis points out that in baptism we are all called to be missionary-disciples. Father Bob's letters identify a number of lessons that are important for all would-be missionary-disciples today. First of all, the letters and anecdotes make it clear that evangelization or mission is a two-way street. It is obvious that Fr. Bob has given needed and generally welcome service to the poor in the medical help that he has provided to so many over the years. It is just as obvious that Fr. Bob has received as much or more from the people he served. Yes, he has been privileged to share his material and spiritual resources with the people he served. At the same time, his letters make it clear that he has received as much or more than he gave. Authentic missionary service demands that we keep our hearts open to receive God's grace and love through the people that we serve.

A second lesson that Fr. Bob offers to aspiring missionary-disciples is his experiential living of interreligious dialogue. Father Bob has lived and served among Muslims in Bangladesh for more than forty years. His encounters reveal the deep respect and reverence he has for Islam. At the same time they reveal his own faith and convictions as a Catholic missionary priest living the gospel among the poor in Bangladesh. Father Bob gives us various illustrations of the openness pointed to by Pope Francis in *The Joy of the Gospel* when he writes: "True openness involves remaining steadfast in one's deepest convictions, clear and joyful in one's own identity, while at the same time being open to understanding those of the other party and knowing that dialogue can enrich each side" (*Evangelii Gaudium* 251).

Another lesson that these letters and stories teach us is that evangelization, mission, is ultimately about encounter. Each anecdote reveals an encounter where all are called to open their hearts to one another; the Christian to the Muslim, the Muslim to the Christian, the old to the young, and the young to the old. It becomes obvious that Fr. Bob's life is lived around being present and encountering, truly encountering, on a constantly deepening level, all the people that he is blessed to meet. It also becomes obvious that it is in the encounter that God becomes somehow present.

The final lesson of this book is that real joy and fulfillment are found in a life lived for others. Pope Francis points out that "when the Church summons Christians to take up the task of evangelization, she is simply pointing to the source of personal fulfillment. For 'here we discover a profound law of reality: that life is attained and matures in the measure that it is offered up in order to give life to others'; this is certainly what mission means" (*Evangelii Gaudium* 10).

I invite you to enjoy the stories and anecdotes and at the same time to grasp how a missionary-disciple's life, lived for others, is its own reward.

Fr. Raymond Finch, M.M.
Superior General
Maryknoll Fathers and Brothers

Preface

Between the ages of six and nineteen my ambition in life changed over a dozen times—from cartoonist to pilot, actor, archeologist, and so on—until the day I telephoned home from college to declare that I intended to become a missioner-priest. Dad answered that call. After hearing me out, he responded as he had to every other wholesome inclination I had ever voiced: "That's fine, son. We're all for it."

There was no question that God was calling me to *missionary* priesthood. In a moment of ecstasy that I experienced on October 31, 1956, in Seattle, Washington, and which continued to thrill my heart until the day I entered the seminary seven and a half months later, I became so conscious of divine love and magnanimity that I longed to give myself entirely to God—even to be promptly dissolved into God if that were possible. Only by becoming a missioner, I felt, could I hope to fulfill that yearning.

In 1964, after seven uneventful but happy years in the seminary, I was duly ordained and received my first assignment to the Philippines. There, on Mindanao, I

This is adapted from the Preface to a previous book by Bob McCahill, *Dialogue of Life: A Christian among Allah's Poor* (Maryknoll, NY: Orbis Books, 1996).

found many opportunities for energetic service among the good, struggling people of the barrios, and other remote areas. But after eleven exhilarating years among the poor of Mindanao, I received word from Maryknoll of the need for volunteers to begin working in Bangladesh.

About Bangladesh I knew little other than that it was near India and that it was constantly in the world news as the site of frequent natural disasters. But the call came at the right moment in my life. It made good sense to me that a missioner would leave one mission—in this case, the Philippines—in order to assist in another, needier mission. And so, in 1975, I left the Philippines behind to enter a new and unfamiliar world.

Until 1947 the place now known as Bangladesh had been a part of India, and then, until 1971, part of Pakistan. In 1971 Bangladesh won its independence. At present in Bangladesh there are more than 165 million people, of whom approximately 86 percent are Muslims and 12 percent are Hindus. It is a crowded place. The area is equivalent to the state of Iowa, but with approximately fifty times the population. Bangladesh is a rich deltic plain. Lush vegetation shoots up quickly from what some regard as the most fertile soil in the world. Most of the people are farm laborers, although the majority of them own no land.

Coming from the Philippines, I found the contrast immediately evident. I had been accustomed to a variety of landscapes, but now forest-covered mountains and cascading streams would be no more than a memory. It appeared to me that the terrain of my new home was almost uninterruptedly, monotonously flat. Markets along the highways seemed to be unvarying conglomerations of low tin sheds. Towns boasted slightly higher buildings, but nothing that would intimidate the most shy villager. I had arrived in winter, and the air was as pleasant as an autumn day in Indiana. There was no hint of the approaching swelter and sweat.

The Holy Cross Fathers and Brothers and Sisters had preceded us to Bangladesh by over a century. They had accomplished a good deal among the small Catholic community (two-tenths of 1 percent of the population). Many Muslims gave them credit for their useful educational and health care institutions. From the ranks of Holy Cross, and from some of the diocesan clergy as well, we found affirmation for our intention to approach Muslims outside of parish structures.

Islam is the state religion of Bangladesh, as could be expected in a nation where six out of seven persons are Muslim. While Islam has always been the predominant religion, the proportion of its adherents has increased steadily over the years. It was our intention from the start to insert ourselves—in some way as yet unknown to us—into the neighborhoods and lives of those people. To live among Bangladeshi Muslims was a project for which there existed no job description. Heretofore the church had placed its personnel in parish houses, convents, and institutions. But no priests or brothers had set out to immerse themselves in the Islamic milieu, that is, to draw water from the same pumps and to bathe in the same ponds as they did, to share everyday laughs and inconveniences with Muslim next-door neighbors. That was the objective in 1975; it remains so four decades later.

When I arrived in Bangladesh, I spent some time

considering how to make myself most useful in service. I chose the sick and disabled as those with whom to involve myself. Attention to sick persons—especially the "hopeless" cases—would, in fact, alleviate the sufferings of only a tiny percentage of people. But, it would also give witness to Christian love for the most abandoned, and to respect for their lives. By living physically quite close to the poor, I intended to make myself available to them in their medical needs. And also simply to show them that we *are* one.

As soon as I began to serve the sick, I was intrigued to see how different their perception of me was from my own perception of myself. Bengali Muslims, I soon learned, do not believe that any benefactor is purely so. That every helper expects a reward pretty well summarizes their attitude. If I were to live among the poor, offer necessary services to persons having serious health problems, and subsequently neither seek nor accept rewards of any sort from them, then perhaps I could help them to understand a form of love that they had not previously experienced, that is, the love of a stranger who seeks no recompense for the benefits he brings. In fact, that is how this apostolate took shape and developed.

In the beginning, having settled in Tangail district, I placed emphasis on serving as many of the sick poor as possible in that locality. After nine years there, at a time when I was well acquainted with health facilities and doctors in the area, and therefore, able to offer competent assistance to many persons, the Spirit moved me to relocate—in order to offer the same witness elsewhere. Thus I moved to Kishoreganj, a hundred miles away, to ease the pain of a few, and to explain to many others who asked me the reasons for my presence among them, and my solicitude for the infirm. Witness, in other words, became as important as service. With the move in location came an accompanying shift in emphasis. Whereas extensive service to the infirm had been my priority, the witness to unselfish love in new communities now took on prominence. Henceforth, I wanted to move into new areas in order to live our signs of Christian discipleship on a broader scale for the full Islamic community: signs of hope for the poor, reconciliation between religious people, and equality of the poor and the rich.

About this book. I am not an author, but rather, a diarist. One would grasp the reason for that admission immediately upon entering the hut I call home. The floor is earthen and damp; the walls are thatched bamboo. There is no ceiling; a bamboo roof slopes up from a height of six feet to a peak at nine feet, then back again to six. For furnishings there is neither desk, typewriter, nor electric lamp. Even coffee, that vital provision for the writer's trade, is in short supply. A bed board and backless stool fill a third of the hut. Whenever I write a letter—as I have to my family every week during my years in Asia—I seat myself on that stool and lean back lightly against the bamboo post by the doorway. (To lean back heavily or abruptly would contribute to loosening the post and weakening the frame of my hut.) Resting my elbow and forearm on the bed board I write in longhand. Usually, I finish before the funny bone in my elbow signals numbness or my feet begin to fall asleep. This arrangement for writing is awkward, impractical, nonconducive to extended periods of reflection, and ultimately fatiguing.

Still, the writing is important in holding on to the daily experiences of mission life. I do it, first, for my own benefit. It seems true to me that a person deeply knows only that which he or she is able, at least in part, to explain. Writing helps me to know what I am thinking. Second, I do it for others' sake. God has placed me in circumstances that few missioners are privileged to enjoy. I should record some of this. Someone may wish to review it and probe it.

Thus, as I bicycle here and there, I occasionally stop to jot down an idea or note a connection that has occurred to me. That practice is not recommended during one's first months in a new locale in Bangladesh because onlook-ers—by whom one is always surrounded—take a dim view of strangers who go around writing notes. He feeds their fancies about the CIA. But there is no other way for me to preserve my thoughts than by scribbling urgently on the backs of scraps of used envelopes the ideas I hope to enlarge on when finally, at day's end, I can seat myself once more to record, from a spine-bending position, the frequently spellbinding experiences of one day in mission.

On Wednesday each week I accompany prospective patients to the regional hospital in Mymensingh. Before the doctors arrive, I scurry to the bishop's house, open a typewriter, and transcribe my notes from the previous week. Then, at month's end, I gather the pages and for-ward the resultant journal from Bangladesh to Maryknoll and on to family members. For many years I have assem-bled some of these notes into an annual letter at Christmas time, which the *National Catholic Reporter* has been in the habit of publishing. From these letters, this present book has been assembled.

The rhythm of life is quite similar no matter where I live in Bangladesh. Thus, the experiences recorded in this little book might as well have happened in one place or another. However, the experiences are not commonplace. In fact, when I sum up these past forty years in Bangladesh, the words *fascinating, illuminating,* and *stimulating* instantly come to my mind.

My customary experience of Muslims—for whatever it is worth—is positive. I admire many Bangladeshi Muslims for reasons that I hope this book will make clear. My prediction is for a future of improving relationships between Muslims and Christians. Moreover, I have reason for the optimism and hope that I feel. The unity among peoples that Jesus prayed for is not, I think, in the dimly glimpsed future. In fact, I believe I hear whispers and see clues of realized oneness here and now. Briefly stated, this Catholic Christian missioner-priest holds that Muslims are good. He hopes that readers of this book will share the same conclusion.

Rejoice with Us!

October 31, 1976
Barisal

Rejoice with us! We five Maryknollers have finished the language course and left the school in Barisal. We have been in Bangladesh for eleven months. This first year and one-half is being spent in trying to understand the good people of Bangladesh and their impressive culture. My efforts at understanding, besides involving me in an intensive language course, motivated me to travel through all nineteen of the districts that constitute this Wisconsin-sized nation. Aside from that, I have been privileged by association with a Muslim religious leader in Barisal to appreciate the spirit of Islam. It is an understatement to say that I respect the Muslims.

You might learn something about the people's value system by reading the following conversation, which is an exchange that I have engaged in at least once a day since arriving in Bangladesh, and oftentimes more than once in the same hour. The Muslim men (for you just don't converse with Muslim women; indeed, you rarely see them) ask: What is your name? Where is your wife? What are you doing here in Bangladesh? How much is your wage? What are your educational qualifications? My answers to those queries tell them who I am: My name is Bob. I am single and celibate. I came to Bangladesh to help people help themselves. I am a volunteer and have no salary. I have a master's degree in education but do not regard it as very important. Answers 2, 3, 4, and 5 literally shock them and lead us into interesting conversations.

During the past four months I have been taking meals in public restaurants. If this conjures up images of soda fountains, tablecloths, air-conditioning, waitresses, and a written menu, you have been grossly misled. I find the people (read: men) easy to meet and engage in conversation. Underneath the reserved and sometimes severe exterior I find them kind, and I have experienced that kindness often. You might say that I like this place.

We realize that we are breaking in to Bangladesh at an unusually good time. Few major disasters have struck during 1976, for example, a month of floods in eastern Bangladesh, a tornado in Faridpur, and the reduction of Ganges River water flow by India. But there has been neither famine, tidal wave, nor war.

Thus, most people feel that this has been a good year for Bangladesh. On the other hand, everybody realizes how quickly the situation could change. The country still lives on the brink of disaster. Families live hand to mouth, from meal to meal. The situation does not foster planning; survival absorbs them.

In conveying this scenario of imminent disaster I am merely reporting reality. I make no mention of what I, or the five of us, intend to do to help the Bangladeshis help themselves to live fuller lives. (The time for speaking about that will come after we have helped.) Nor do I suggest the key role that the United States could play in making jobs for Bangladeshis so they can work, eat, and live a bit more humanely. (But if anybody asks, I'll surely tell him why I think the United States holds the key to Bangladesh's survival.)

Remember Me,
From Half a World Away?

October 12, 1977
Tangail

Remember me, from half a world away? Let me tell you what I've been up to during 1977. Then it'll be your turn to tell me about the things that have occupied your minds and hearts since last you wrote.

Since January 1977, I have been living in Tangail, a city of 30,000 people, sixty miles north of Dacca. I live in a single room, which I rent for four dollars a month, eat in tea stalls for seventy cents a day, seek help from countless people to express myself in correct Bangla (Everybody is "Mr. Bob's" teacher), explain to all who ask what motivates me to live among them, namely, I love people, so I want to live among them; I love Allah, so I try to give myself completely to him through celibacy and prayer. (By the way, for working among Muslims I cannot imagine a greater advantage than the celibate life; the Muslims regard celibacy as, simply, a miracle.) People sometimes ask me if I know any place where their sickness will be

3

treated without cost. Few of the people who receive treatment are cured, but most of them receive the joy of knowing that someone has hope for them. I have a hunch that what they most appreciate about my little service is that I care about their welfare.

A number of you, my friends, have sent financial help for the sake of the poorest in Bangladesh. You did a good work. I have channeled that money to a couple of communities who use funds carefully: (1) The Missionary Sisters of Charity, who pick up the sick and dying from the streets, feed and clothe the neediest; and (2) a nameless community of Christians who run a large clinic near the Dacca railroad station, where destitute people congregate. I do not work at either place but know for sure that your offering is well used by them.

Maybe some of you would be happier if I were to be, personally, the one to put food, medicine, clothing, or money directly into the hands of the needy. So far, it has not been necessary for me to deal in money and things; and I hope that I will never have to. When I came here two years ago, my single intention was to assist the poor by any possible means, in whatever way the Lord would lead me to do. My present understanding of the needs of the people leads me to feel that the best I can do for them is to make my respect for them so clear that they will feel their dignity. I like the Bangladeshis. I want them to feel that. I hope they catch some of my joy at being among them. I want to be their friend. Nothing more.

It is hard to be a friend to anyone you are giving money to. You can be his benefactor, the guy who saves his life, his protector, his security. But when you are holding the money you cannot easily be a friend to anyone in need. And, maybe, since there are about 140 other international organizations already at work trying to alleviate poverty in Bangladesh, it won't hurt if Maryknollers in Bangladesh concern themselves with just being friends to the poor. At any rate, this is what we are trying to do. Help us with your prayers. May the peace of Allah be showered on you!

Postscript: At the end of last year's letter to you I mentioned that "If anybody asks, I'll surely tell him why I think the United States holds the key to Bangladesh's survival." Some of you did ask, because you wanted to do more than pray for the poor, more than send your missionaries to live among the poor. What more can a person do to help the poor? It seems to me that the first step we should take is to make the effort to be accurately informed about U.S. business and government involvement abroad. U.S. business and government policies are not sufficiently responsive to a world filled with acute want. We, as a nation, could do a lot more than we are doing to assure humane treatment and humane conditions for all human beings. Some might deny that, and others might simply want not to consider it, but my observation is that American business and government have a huge impact on the lives of four billion people. One further observation: We can influence those policies for the better if we'll take the trouble to be accurately informed.

I Wish You Joy

November 30, 1978
Tangail

As-salaam alaikum! Peace be to you! That's the way the Bangladeshi Muslim greets persons of goodwill. Persons like yourself. *As-salaam alaikum*!

You already know that Bangladesh has a lot of people living on a little bit of land. A recent survey says that 48

percent of our farmers are landless. That means that many own no land, not even the ground under the family's hut, and that others own less than one-half acre of land. Who can support a family of six or seven persons on half an acre of land or less? No one can. It bothers me that I am not helping to solve their basic problem: landlessness/ unemployment. For the present, however, it is my joy to be serving some of them in matters of health. The service amounts to no more than a sign, seen by a few, that there is such a thing as disinterested love, even among mere men. If I could (and I can't) send you a pair of photos showing four-year-old Shahajahan, one photo from before treatment (when he weighted twelve pounds and had marasmic kwashiorkor, pulmonary tuberculosis, pneumonia, urinary tract infection, anemia, and worms), and another photo from after treatment (he is playful and laughing), you'd be pleased to see how six weeks on good food and simple medicine can radically revive the near-dead.

A poet in this poetry-loving part of the world wrote about the terrible dilemma facing too many of this country's mothers:

> Decide, Mother;
> Who goes without?
> Is it Rama, the strongest
> Who may not need it that day?
> Or Bala, the weakest
> Who may not need it much longer?
> Or perhaps Sita
> Who may be expendable?
> Decide, Mother.
> Kill a part of yourself

As you resolve the dilemma.
Decide, Mother.
Decide …
And hate.

A few months ago a friend traveled to Bangladesh from his home in South America. He told me that the poor of that continent are as bad off as the poor of Bangladesh. That is poor indeed, and it makes me angry. Too many human beings cannot, and do not, live *human* lives. They *can* survive.

It'd be nice if I'd write something lighter to you. But, as a matter of fact, there's nothing light on my mind. This is my fourteenth year overseas, and I still do not understand *how* the poor of the "developing nations" resist death. Considering their living conditions, it edifies me *that* they resist death. If that statement lacks optimism, so be it. I find it somewhat hard to be euphoric while children are hungry. Meanwhile, your newspaper probably tells you that Bangladesh is having another good year. … These observations are enough to make me sober about my own standard of living, thoughtful about my own lifestyle, and angry about the whole gamut of injustices, on global, national, and village levels, that work against God because they are working against men and women. So much for the things that meet one's eye in Bangladesh.

Among the 84 million Bangladeshis, 90 percent are Muslims. Just as significant as their Islamic faith is the Sufi (mystical) influence that permeates the peoples' religious feeling. There is a Sufi gathering, called simply a "meeting," attended occasionally by Muslim men. It is a spiritual songfest that lasts all night long and resembles a Christian Cursillo closing, or a charismatic prayer meeting. This Sufi event, and various other Sufi practices, must have something to do with the unlettered farmers' unshakable faith in Allah, and the delight they experience in singing or hearing sung his praise. I thank Allah for the relief that this mystical tendency gives to the poor. The spiritual vitality of the struggling villager is something that doesn't meet the eye. The human person is more than he appears to be.

Do tell me: what have you got to say for *your* good self? I wish you joy,

I Love the Poor and Respect Islam

November 22, 1979
Tangail

On Thursdays, I accompany patients from the village to a large charity hospital at Mirzapur, nineteen miles from Tangail, by bus. Then, on Fridays, I take patients to various hospitals in Dacca, sixty miles away. I usually stay overnight Friday in Dacca with the Holy Cross Brothers. They are kind men.

One Sunday per month I celebrate Mass with the Christian nurses at Mirzapur Hospital. That is the extent of my pastoral ministry among Christians in this Muslim country.

Once in a while visitors from abroad drop in on us. Those who bring a dozen chocolate bars I recall most vividly. Man does not live on potatoes alone. ...

Once a year I manage to travel to India. "Mother India" surrounds Bangladesh, and it is possible to go there by bus. Earlier this year I participated in the Consultation on Christian–Muslim Relations, held near the Taj Mahal. Whatever one learns about India helps one to understand Bangladesh better.

Regarding the apostolate in Tangail, you might wonder why I decided to concentrate my attention on the sick-poor in the villages. I was struck by the fact that the poor do not seek professional medical attention, even if it is free. I recalled that Jesus, in the finest description of his work found in the Acts of the Apostles, "went about doing good and healing." I was moved to do likewise.

I spend no time working for conversions. I love the poor and respect Islam. So does God. I believe that Muslims can be and are saved within Islam. So I make no effort to convince Muslims to profess Christianity. What I do is try to live a Christian life in the midst of Muslims. Each member of the group, in his own way, is trying to do likewise, and supports the others in their efforts. We trust that Allah is using us to move hearts toward him. I haven't yet met a Muslim who really wants to *hear* a Christian's views on Jesus. (They have their own idea about Jesus.) But I have met hundreds who appreciate very much seeing someone who follows Jesus. Therefore, that's what I spend my time trying to be—a follower of Jesus. Your prayers do help me. Thank you! In the name of Allah, the Compassionate, the Merciful, ...

Postscript: I was out in a village today looking for the sick. So many *are* sick. It occurs to me that all these sick and suffering Muslims and Hindus (there are no Christians here) are the great ones in God's kingdom, here and now. They are the poor, the suffering, the lowly, to whom the kingdom belongs. There is no chance that they will not be saved. God is neither cruel nor dull. He would have to be one or the other if he'd refuse everlasting joy and comfort to people who are so miserable now. My conviction is based on common sense. Living among the poor helps to straighten out my thinking about God. Anyway, it seems so to me.

Love Is the Only Charism Allah Gives Me

October 31, 1980
Tangail

There is a question I hear frequently from people I meet on the trail as I go about looking for sick persons to help. It means, "What were you doing (in the village you just visited)?"

If you were to ask me the same question I could answer in all the following ways. I've been:

Thinking that what I'm doing for the sick poor is comparable to a drop in the ocean, that it is too little to be doing for needy persons, too limited in scope, too inefficient. ... But, that it's a good thing I'm doing it.

Admiring the stoicism and heroism of the poor during three weeks of flooding in August while their homes were uninhabitable and their meals few and far between.

Consoling persons like the widowed mother of Bashi, a vivacious fifteen-year-old girl who died three hours after a cobra, flushed out by rising flood waters, bit her.

Giving gladly to a steady stream of women, mostly widows or divorced, toting infants and wearing ragged *sharis*, gathered at our door to ask, in Allah's name, for a handful of rice. (Sometimes I invite trios of them inside, seat them, pour water over their right hands, and offer them puffed rice with molasses. To treat "beggars" as guests bends their minds.)

Staggering along a crowded street cradling in my arms a filthy, abandoned old man whom people stop to stare at but not to touch.

Riding bicycle to the villages and then having a Bengali tell me, "Sometimes people stay up until one o'clock at night just trying to understand why a rich American rides a bike instead of a car, and wears sandals instead of high-heeled shoes."

Carrying the corpse of a neighbor boy to the cemetery and being informed at the cemetery mosque that "You are not a Muslim. Therefore you cannot pray with us for the boy."

Receiving invitations to the hut of Yakob Ali, where, on occasion, he invites me to feed on puffed rice and fresh fruit while his family of eight takes pleasure watching me.

There are few things in life that I enjoy as much as eating with the poor, even though it sometimes results in my "growing" a tapeworm.

Marketing in a muddy bazaar where the person who refuses to haggle over prices gets stung.

Consulting a *moulana* (an Islamic religion teacher) who interprets *ahadith* (the sayings and doings of the Prophet Muhammad) for me, and who tells me his dreams whenever they have anything to do with me.

Laughing at the antics of infants and children before adverting to the fact that adults think I'm goofy for being so amused.

Studying Bangla language a bit less than I should, but nevertheless communicating well with people, not because I'm a language expert but because I love them. (Love is the only charism Allah gives me. And it's enough.)

Praying almost always. There's a constant undercurrent of longing for God in my mind and heart that gives me peace even when I'm agitated.

Welcoming frequent visits from Jamal Sheikh, who walks seven miles to bring to me sick persons from his area. Typically for a Bengali, he is married, has five children, no land, no regular work, and lives in a bamboo-and-grass hut. Not so typically, he is interested in helping others, and does so.

Thanks for every encouraging word you've sent this past year, either to me, or directly to Allah for me.

Postscript: Five years ago, I left the Philippines. If you've ever wondered whether I still think of the Filipino people, the answer is yes, I do, often. I have plenty to remind me about my home for eleven years. Monthly reports tell me of the fear and pain experienced daily by too many Filipinos. I read with a heavy heart reports of the military's abuse of poor, innocent citizens. I have the impression that what was told to me in 1975 is just as true today for lots of good, simple people: "Father, the Japanese soldiers occupied our Province during the Second World War. They were harsh, but not as mean as the Philippines' troops who harass us now. We never feared the invaders as much as we now fear 'our own.'" I pray daily for the Filipinos and for all who, like them, are living in fear. I believe there's no human condition as nearly like Hell as is living in fear of violence at the hands of arrogant and unpredictable bullies. So, please pray for the Filipinos, Koreans, Argentinians, Somalians, and others whose Hell is now.

Looking for Ways Just to Make Them Smile

October 31, 1981
Tangail

Greetings from Bangladesh, where you have a 44-year-old, wiry, graying, happy, chocolate-deprived but peanut-butter addicted, bicycle-riding missioner friend.

October 31 is a special date for me. That's when, in 1956, I received from God an unmistakable call to become a priest-missioner. To be what God urges me to be has been my single aim in life since then. I'd be pleased if others were to look into this way of life for themselves. Not because I want Maryknoll to have more members, but because I like to see people happy. I happen to believe that living among, and being of service to, the poor (i.e., my description of mission in the modern world) is a ticket to earthly happiness. I have a hunch that any young American who would spend a few weeks living and learning in Bangladesh would feel his life changed. He might even decide to offer his life to the poor. I reckon that would be the happiest decision of his life. (I don't see lots of evidence that Americans are really happy, in spite of an impressive per capita income.)

Six years ago, Maryknoll asked for volunteers from among its members in the missions to open up a new unit in Bangladesh. Five of us came. This December will mark the end of our sixth year, so we are now evaluating our work. The basic question that the evaluation must answer, as I see it, is rather simple: Should Maryknoll continue in Bangladesh, and why? To which I reply a resounding YES. The reason I give is that here our small fraternity of missioners has the opportunity to personally serve and befriend truly poor people.

Bangladesh is a good place for missioners to live, it seems to me. I believe that Christians—and especially missioners—are sent by God to the nations of the world primarily for the poor who live there. The poor of all religions, or of no religion, are our priority concern. It is by being with and for the poor that we proclaim the Good News to all classes of people. The message is that God loves and cares for the neediest among us.

The needs of the poor specify what I do here. Many are sick; I attempt to bring some of them to medical treatment. Now that I've been doing this work for a few years, it is apparent to me both: (a) how little God needs me here (i.e., I'm scratching the surface); and (b) how good it is that he's got me here (i.e., doing something beats doing nothing). A bonus discovery, made while accompanying the sick, the lame, and the blind to hospitals, has to do with the "problem of evil" in the world. I marvel at how so many people can be disabled and still keep on working. I ask myself: Why does God "allow" them to struggle so desperately? An answer comes to me: People are sick and struggling

16

so that those who are healthier and more secure will help them.

So, I'm trying to live as if the poor were my own sisters and brothers. The time, energy, and wee bit of money I spend on them probably doesn't renew their hope or increase their love for life as much as does the simple fact that I like them and like to be around them. To tell the truth, I'm often looking for ways just to make them smile. You, by your prayers, letters, and other gifts, give me reason to smile.

Postscript: Let me mention to you something that's bothering me. Newscasts beamed this way from the United States speak optimistically about space exploration. Many of my countrymen seem enthusiastic about this new, exciting aspect of modern life. They cannot be persons who have seen other human beings in need of food, medicine, or shelter.

Space exploration at this moment in history disturbs me. The astronomical sums of money spent by Americans on probes into space become obscene when compared with the needs of the poor on planet Earth. A rich nation can dare to experiment in space only when people of all races and places are eating enough each day. Those same billions of dollars if spent instead on research into basic needs and employment-creation in the poorest countries would go a long way toward making this a better world.

Every time I see hungry people—that is daily—I also think of the money, talent, and effort being spent by Americans on space. It pains me. Meanwhile, persons just like you and me are hurting and hungry. Americans are simply wrong to spend money in space while hundreds of millions of God's beloved ones on earth remain locked in destitution. For us to pretend that the hungry, sick, and inadequately housed are not our responsibility shows a failure not only of the heart to respond in mercy but also a failure of the intelligence to recognize how much better this world would be for all of us if the poorest had more in life.

Americans can and must do much more for the world's poor. Shall we?

The Key to Paradise Is Love for the Poor

October 31, 1982
Tangail

There's an informal greeting used by Bengali friends, meaning "How are you?" My hope is that you can answer it as Bangladeshi Muslims do, that is, "Allah keeps me well."

Several years ago, as many of you may recall, I began wrestling with the question: What should this rich Christian do with the opportunity he has to live among the poor? The answer I arrived at was:

a. Share as much in their condition of poverty as my health will allow.

b. Live physically in their midst.

c. Live for them, at their service; spend myself for them.

There is no more exciting news I have to report to you this year than that Allah continues to move Jake, Doug, and myself along this path and that it's exhilarating.

Archbishop Michael of Dacca, who sponsors our staying in Bangladesh and within whose jurisdiction we are in mission among Muslims, recently asked each one of us to answer two questions: What have you been doing in Tangail? And, what have you been trying to accomplish by it?

I replied: "The original purpose I had in coming to Bangladesh was to be of service to the poor. I feel that is a proper role for a missioner. Christians are supposed to be servants of the poor; missioners are supposed to be exemplary Christians. While I do not claim to be an exemplary Christian, I do have that as my goal. I am trying to be a Christian in the midst of the Muslim poor. In pursuit of that objective, I find it fitting to dedicate myself to helping the sick, who, because of their poverty, have no hope of receiving medical assistance.

I love the sick-poor for whom I work. I believe that many of the people whom I serve and even some of the middle class who see me serving the poor understand that I love the poor. When I began this work several years ago there was widespread suspicion of my motives. At present, however, a great number of people believe that the service I render is from the heart and is disinterested. That is, they understand that I am not using my service as bait, nor striving for the conversion of anyone to Christianity. Being and behaving as a Christian brother among the poor Muslims are my whole purpose.

I want to share as much as I can in the condition of the poor. The comfort, convenience, and security that are mine for the taking, simply because I am an American citizen, remind me that other people do not enjoy such things.

Comfort: Whenever I choose to take them, I can eat three square meals a day.

Convenience: Almost at will, I can arrange for a day off. I also have the freedom to leave this place for an extended vacation. Security: I have the assurance that I'll never die for want of medical care, housing, or food.

Gratitude is like background music running through my mind and heart. I thank the All Generous One constantly for his gifts. The freedom he gives me is an immense gift. I am even free to give up some of my privileges and to offer them back to the Giver. I thank the Lord for giving me an ever-stronger desire to adhere to the poor … even though, it seems to me, the more I do the less it matters. What does matter? I think it matters more that I am a sign of God's love for the poor and a sign that (the Christian) God loves the Muslims than that I'm accomplishing anything for the sick-poor. Excuse the analogy, but I'm sort of a sacrament, accepted with joy and befriended by the poor, while being rejected by some few "orthodox" Muslims who do not like to see a Christian exemplifying the mercy they talk about. "There is a key for everything, and the key of Paradise is love for the poor." That Christian sentiment was enunciated by Muhammad, the Prophet of Islam.

By the way, some of you may be disappointed that I haven't been sending photos to you as I used to do. Formerly, I had a peach of a camera, but it was plucked one day along with lots of other articles in the fraternity house. Since then, we have replaced some items: for example, we now have a slightly less powerful radio than the one that was lifted. Shall I replace the camera? It is not clear to me that its usefulness is in proportion to the effort required to protect it. As you know, we did not come here in order to stand guard over our goods. Tell me, if you were in my sandals, what would you do?

My prayer and wish for you are that starting now, you'll be a raving success in life, that is, that every time you set out to make somebody feel better, they will indeed feel better.

Postscript to fellow-pilgrims: A letter came my way not long ago in which a friend asked: "Bob, what can we do for the missions besides praying?" In my reply I didn't speak about money. Money has its place in helping the missions, but perhaps enough has already been said about that. One practical effort is clearly more important, as I see things. The best way for an American to help the missions, that is, to help the people who live in this country and in all the other countries to which the church sends missioners, is, in my opinion, to try to move the U.S. government to use its wealth better. The resources of our nation include scientific expertise and an unmatched capacity for research, as well as great natural resources. A grossly unfair amount of those resources is spent on armaments, military preparedness, and on the space program (which is also, alas, militarily useful). People of goodwill should band together to influence the government to change its priorities. There are a number of fine organizations already in existence in the Western nations whose membership thinks more of the precarious existence of hundreds of millions of the world's poor than of the misconceived "security" of the rich, powerful nations. Those organizations should be joined. Intelligent discussion should be constantly engaged in. Resolutions to strive for peace and a better distribution of the world's resources of talent and treasure should be worked for.

Missioners love the people among whom they work. Perhaps there is nothing better that an American could do to help those good people than to be a determined, though peace-filled, agitator of the powers that be.

Showing God's Love, Especially to the Poorest

October 31, 1983
Tangail

You may have noticed that I write to you every year around October 31. Why? Because on that date in 1956 I was overwhelmingly attracted to God; I received an unmistakable call to give myself entirely to the Lord. I celebrate that unforgettable date each year by greeting friends.

What are you doing here? That's a question Bengalis continue to ask me even though I've been living for nearly seven years in the same small city in north-central Bangladesh. I reply: "I try to help people who are sick and poor."

Why do that? They ask. I answer, "Because Jesus, my Model, did it."

My purpose here continues to be simply to live as a Christian among Muslims, showing God's love, especially to the poorest.

I used to think that the surprised reaction of Muslims to this somewhat friendly missioner was due to the novelty of having a foreigner dwelling among them. Then, an educated villager instructed me about the lasting effects of colonialism. "We Bengalis think that Englishmen ('Englishmen' is what we call all white foreigners) are primarily interested in women and dancing. In our dramas and plays, Englishmen are portrayed as swallowing women, and as looking down on us Bengalis." He concluded by offering an evaluation: "There are two things you Mary-knoll Brothers have done that amaze us. One is that, in your dealings with women, you are absolutely trustworthy. The other is that you treat the poor with respect. I tell you clearly, in these two matters you have succeeded in changing the minds of some of us about foreigners."

Before coming to Bangladesh in 1975, a veteran missioner to this area warned us: "Unfortunately, you will not be able to work with women; Muslims will not trust you." I am particularly glad, therefore, about the reputation for trustworthiness in dealing with women.

Progressively, it has been dawning on me that my efforts have to do with more than helping and healing the sick. I also invite and inspire trust. How? I ride to faraway villages on a bike (i.e., my little charism), offer to help the sick-poor, listen attentively to those who approach me, and stick with the serious patients until their treatment is concluded. People here have apparently never seen this sort of concern before. At first sight, it seems incomprehensible to them. They ask one another: What's in it for him? What's his angle? However, after a while (i.e., years), word has gotten around that this foreign chap genuinely cares about suffering people; one doesn't have to bribe him; he won't turn you away; he'll spend time, energy, and money (sometimes as much as 40 cents US) to help you find treatment; he expects nothing in return; go ahead and send your child or sister or wife with him because he is like a brother or a maternal uncle to them.

It is literally thrilling for me to win the trust of the poor. Now, many of them invite me into their hut-homes, request me to share their food, bring me along with them to religious festivals, ask me to bless them when they are sick, and when they are well, expect me to name their babies, pray for me, and tell me jokes.

They know that I am a Christian and that my faith is not a threat to theirs.

Recently I received some feedback from a middle-class Muslim: "What can be done for this poor country of mine, Brother Bob? There is so much poverty! But you, Brother, have done the only thing that can be done: you are serving the poorest people. If you had tried to work among the middle-class or the rich, they would not have accepted you. But because you have gone to the poorest, all the people love you, both the rich and the poor. I am speaking from my chest!"

It is more than possible that my friend exaggerates. (What else are friends for?) But if there is any truth in what he says, credit must go first to Allah, and then to my mother and father. Briefly analyzed: I imitate Mom when I feel compassion for folks who are hurt; I imitate Dad when I take the initiative to do something about it. I, too, speak from my heart when I thank Mom and Dad for living for us (their four children) so that we might live for others. By the way, this is their anniversary, too: Golden Wedding.

What are you doing there? Are you celebrating any anniversaries?

With thanks to Allah for your friendship, your brother.

Postscript for fellow-pilgrims: It's a Friday as I write this letter, the day on which many of the village poor stream into town, moving from door to door to ask for a bit of rice-grain to take home. These good people do not take meals for granted.

I don't mean to sound grim, but these are persons who have nothing more to lose of material wealth. Yet, they smile, in return for yours. They can laugh and sing, not because they feel physically secure, but in spite of insecurity. They simply must, and, therefore do, trust mightily in Allah, who is indestructible. That trust gives them security.

There is nothing romantic about poverty. When I observe that the poor have saving graces, it is not in order to glorify destitution. Rather, it is to say that Allah can do surprisingly beautiful things in the hearts of people who suffer.

The poor do not realize how impressive they are to me as they carry on under frightening, depressing conditions. They edify me by being cheerful when I would be anxious. It would be a mistake to imagine that this Catholic-Christian missioner-priest is not immensely enriched by his contact with faithful Muslims. I see Allah at work in them.

There is nothing that I would accept in trade for this way of life. I wish you, for a lifetime, the same sort of joy I experience while living with and for the poor. Let's keep reminding one another that God cannot be outdone in generosity. Therefore, the truly wise ones will give themselves to others radically … in that way to experience deeper joy in their own lives, now, a hundredfold.

What Actions Are Most Excellent?

October 31, 1984
Tangail

It is reported that the Prophet of Islam, Muhammad, once said: "What actions are most excellent? To gladden the heart of a human being, to feed the hungry, to help the afflicted, to lighten the sorrow of the sorrowful, and to remove the wrongs of the injured." I am daily and deeply grateful to God for having given me one more year of life (number 47) with its many opportunities to gladden, to feed, to help, and to lighten the sorrows of others.

Probably this year's most surprising discovery has been that blind people, of whom Bangladesh has hundreds of thousands, wish to have their photographs taken. Ayub came to get his photo the other day. I had a nice one to present to him. He smiled broadly when I placed it in his hands. His companion, the boy who leads him around the town and villages, exclaimed, "Fine photo!" Ayub chuckled and squirmed with pleasure as others gathered to view his portrait. He cannot see it, of course. But others do see it and offer their comments about it. That photo indicates to Ayub something about his value. It's as if I had told him, "You're important; I like you." Sometimes a photograph is like a hug.

It's easy to admire blind people. They instruct me by their good example. Every few days I pass by Banu, who sits at the roadside begging. Her naked three-year-old daughter, Fori, plays in the dirt beside her. Last week,

I greeted the blind mother and her seeing child. Banu responded in her customary, cheerful way. Then she called my attention to the torn *sharee* she was wearing. I cajoled her: "Listen, Banu. Already it's the hot season; torn clothing is advantageous: you'll be cooler and more comfortable that way." Banu's face lit up. She giggled merrily. Such a good-humored lady. Blind since birth, owning nothing. And always ready to laugh.

Some persons are so grievously ill that the best way I know to help them is by speaking a word of truth. Last month, I admitted Bilayet to a hospital, but within one week they released him. They could not test him; he should return to the village in order to die at home. Bilayet draped his arm over my neck while we descended the stairway, and sighed: "I'm so weak … couldn't eat all week long." I spoke of Allah's love for him, assured him that Allah knows what he's going through, and that he

28

is a good person. Among those truths the last one was the most astounding for him to hear. No one ever tells a black, illiterate, threadbare, and shoeless, physically broken villager that he is a good person. Although Bilayet was beyond smiling, I believe he treasured until the hour of his death those three little words: *You are good.*

You may have read about the floods in Bangladesh this year. Recently, I was slogging through thigh-deep waters in order to visit Amena, an ailing mother. It was slippery going. A crowd of onlookers watched expectantly for me to fall. I didn't disappoint them. As I lurched backward into muddy water, do you imagine that I heard expressions of sympathy or even politely muffled laughter? Not so. I heard, rather, guffaws, and observed that even the sick lady was grinning. I'd touched her funny bone. Sometimes, the good I accomplish is not the good I'd intended.

Multiply the above-mentioned incidents by a few hundred or thousand and you'll have an accurate-enough idea of what one Catholic missioner priest in a Muslim-majority country has been doing. I try not to exaggerate the joy God gives me through the sick-poor. But, as a matter of fact, I'm truly happy, in love with persons who suffer without grumbling, and more in need of them than they are in need of me.

Praise belongs to Allah!

Postscript for fellow pilgrims: Sometimes, I accuse myself: Man, what are you doing!? When are you going to start helping to change structures that oppress people? You're so wrapped up in people's lives that you haven't the time or energy to grapple with the big issues. Then I beat my scrawny chest, admit my deficiencies, and view myself with calm amusement. Anyway (I say to myself), who knows? Maybe God uses even my wee efforts to help transform oppressive structures.

Helping the poor is a work recommended by all the great religions. "Helping the poor" is also an expression so trite that I used to think it described just one among many laudable human activities. No longer do I underestimate that work. The promise of another Great Prophet is fulfilled: When you give a party, invite the poor, the crippled, the lame, and the blind. They have no means of repaying you. In that way lies real happiness for you.

Allah Is Closer to You Than Your Jugular Vein

October 31, 1985
Tangail

The Lord is with you. Or, as our Muslim sisters and brothers say: Allah is closer to you than your jugular vein.

Bangladesh continues to be a fine place for meeting heroes, or, as in so many instances, heroines. Shukimon (her name means "Happy") is a widow, aged 26 years, and mother of two girls who need more to eat. She often skips the meals that people for whom she works give her and carries the food home to Oruna and Asiya on a banana leaf. I met her on a trail, and referring to the badly torn blue rag she'd worn daily for months, I asked if she owns another sharee. "*Na!*" she sang cheerfully, the way Bengalis do when describing personally desperate conditions. I bought her a new one for 80 takas ($3 US) and pleaded with her not to tell anyone from whom she got the new cloth. She promised she'd be quiet … to protect me.

Frequently I meet persons who, delightful to say, put me to shame. I'd just gotten out of a hospital where I'd undergone an operation and spent a week recovering. Friends assured me they had prayed to Allah to make me well and commended me for daring. Soon afterward, a 25-year-old fellow named Hossain came to me for help. He was bent at the waist so that his back was fixed at a 90 degrees angle to his legs. The hospital surgeons were not keen on operating. But Hossain insisted: "Let happen what will happen. That is up to Allah. You must try to straighten me out." During eight weeks in that dreary institution I did not once observe Hossain despairing,

despite the fact that he had never been so far away from home and friends, was enduring multiple discomforts, and was not at all improved by the major operation. No one called him brave, and none congratulated him for the risk he'd taken. The poor don't praise one another for grit, nor heap words of encouragement on those who expose themselves to danger. It is enough that they share that same condition.

At the village home of friends I came across a girl named Romoni. As their hut lacked furniture, she fetched a stool from the neighbor's house for me to sit on. We conversed while she stirred rice. Dignified, shy, and pleasant, Romoni was the typical Bengali young lady. The next day she managed somehow to get a bit of goat meat, which she cooked and sent to me. The gesture touched me: Bengal villagers are lucky to eat meat once in two months. Three weeks later, I bicycled again to their home and was stunned to see the freshly filled grave of my generous young friend. She had committed suicide three days earlier. No one could say why.

The poor are easy to admire. Every one of them has a story worth hearing. My brother Dick visited Bangladesh last March, witnessed their material poverty, and marveled: "The kids are so happy. They're always laughing." I'm glad he saw that. On the other hand, a glimpse of people's hidden pain comes from the reports of an astounding number of suicides throughout the country. Many of the suicides are by females between the ages of 10 and 25.

The One God of Muslims and Christians is merciful and compassionate. A line I once heard in a movie expresses rather well the response I hope that One will keep on making through me to persons who are on the verge: "What then must we do? We must give love to every person whom God places in our path."

This has been the niftiest ten years of my life ... thankfully.

Postscript for fellow pilgrims: This missioner in Bangladesh cannot imagine a mission approach to Muslims that is more revealing of Christ's love than the approach of One who came not to be served but to serve, and to give. The approach is this: I seek out the sick-poor in their village homes, invite them to accompany me to hospitals, and make myself available to help any persons who come to me in need of healing. What, then, do Muslims think of all this? Yakob, a long-time friend, spoke with frank concern recently, "Your health has broken." Perhaps he and others have a hunch that I love them and that I believe they're worth spending myself for.

You probably know that many Muslims feel threatened by Christian missioners. They fear we will use our money to convert them to Christianity. One of the targets of our efforts for the sick-poor is the entire Muslim community. For here in their midst they observe a fraternity of Christian missioners who have been befriending Muslims for nearly a decade without ever suggesting conversion. If Muslims require evidence that Christian missioners do not regard them as a damned mass, but that, rather, we respect Muslims and their Islamic faith, then evidence is here. In fact, many Muslims see that evidence and wonder: "Is it possible that followers of diverse faiths are meant by Allah merely to befriend, and not to conquer, one another?"

Allah Makes Happy Those Who Serve the Needy

October 31, 1986
Kishoreganj

This year, I did something that perhaps a few of you did also. I moved. After nine fine years in Tangail of helping the poor in ways they want to be helped I judged that the signs of love for the poor and respect for their faith had been made for a sufficient duration of time by this missioner. It was time to move on to another place in order to make the same signs to new persons.

"Do come to Kishoreganj; we welcome a brother who will live among us in poverty and chastity." Those words of welcome from one respected citizen provided the invitation I needed in order to transfer to Kishoreganj (pronounced: *key-shore-ganj*), a district town 100 miles east of my former abode, populated by 100,000 people, approximately 90 percent Muslims and 10 percent Hindus.

In the new place, I rented a room for $6 per month, furnished it with a single-burner kerosene stove, a candle-holder, a clay water jar, a washpan, plate and glass, a sleeping mat, and a wardrobe as elaborate as my surroundings. Doug kindly supplied me with a slightly leaky pressure cooker; he knows I have not the patience to deal with any other sort of cooking. Then I set out to get to know the Kishoreganjis.

Among the persons of good will whom I met were Rowshon, a weary but cheerful rickshaw-puller who found a room for me to rent; Kader, who fulfills all the religious observances and cautions me, "We are watching you"; Hashem, who led me to see a sick person on my first day in town; Mannan, a teacher who tried to convince me that "Woman is the smallest tail of a man"; Nurun Begum, the gracious and competent directress of the local boys' orphanage; Mahbuhul, chairman of the town's Islamic burial society, which has buried 118 unclaimed bodies during the past four years; Sharifuddin, who enjoys narrating the history he has witnessed since 1900; Kafil, a poet and revolutionary; Shofiqul, who proudly showed me around the town's largest mosque and confided; "I love America"; and Francis, a Christian recently arrived in town who uses a Muslim name and tries to live anonymously among his neighbors.

"Who are you? What do you do?" the people want to know. I explain: "I am Brother Bob, a Catholic Christian missioner. I am here to serve the sick-poor. Service to the needy and love for all persons is my religion. Christians believe that Allah makes happy those who serve the needy." Implied in my reply is a message for any who wish to understand it: "This Christian missioner is your brother. I wish you well. I appreciate your faith and your culture. There is nothing about you that I seek to change except that which you also wish changed. I will gladly try to help you free yourselves from whatever debilitates you, that is, free you for living useful and happy lives."

There are no other foreigners in Kishoreganj. Not now. But between 1916 and 1930 the Nazarene Christian Mission of Kansas City, Missouri, maintained a girls' high school in this unlikely place. Only Allah knows what were and are the effects of that mission effort. One thing is clear, however. There is fellow-feeling in Kishoreganj. Did the Nazarene Mission contribute to that attitude? Or is it solely due to the strivings of Muslims and Hindus to live harmoniously together? Or is it for reasons I have yet to discover? The place fascinates me.

So do the people. I wish you could meet many of them. Like Chaytali. Her age is fourteen years, and she is the last of fourteen children, three of whom survive. Both parents are gone. Chaytali stands five feet tall, weighs 64 pounds, has fine features, a light complexion, and a winning smile.

Six months ago, someone humiliated her so severely that she wanted to die, for which purposely she drank some nitric acid from a jeweler's shop. The attempt failed, but as a result of it she can no longer swallow food and lives on milk whenever she can get some. "I want to eat rice again!" she declares. First, though, she'll have to have some work done on her esophagus. I volunteered to be her brother; she prefers to call me "Dada" (Grandpa). She assures me that she never went to school and is "dumb." However, she is anything but that. I marvel at the intelligence and resourcefulness of this sweet, scrawny Bengali lass. Now she wants to live and not to die. She can use a little help from her friends.

May God give you, too, the joy of helping friends in need in your mission place. ...

Postscript: Many thanks for letters, news clippings, and other forms of encouragement you've sent to tickle me. Because of your thoughtfulness, I get the best of two worlds, that is, friends there and friends here.

Not long ago, I arrived unannounced at the home of Toyob. Within minutes his two married daughters had sliced up a pair of mangoes (the fruit of kings and the king of fruits) and presented them to me in the family dish. That gift, coming from an extended family living in three mud-and-straw huts, made my day. Having little is no obstacle to giving much.

I'm grateful to these friends, too.

Hospitality . . . a Way to Find a Place in One Another's Heart

October 31, 1987
Kishoreganj

I suppose that when people think of Bangladesh they think of food, or the lack of it. In fact, there is plenty of food here. The people simply lack the cash to buy enough of it. The main reasons for hunger, it seems to me, are underpaid labor and underemployment.

You may be interested to hear about some of the ways that food touches on my efforts to give Christian witness and service to Bengali Muslims.

Neighboring women drop by my bamboo hut, stand on the earthen veranda peering inside, and ask me what foods I'm preparing. They think it's amazing and amusing that I don't cook spicy foods. For them, that's life in the slow lane. An English author I once read claimed it is bad etiquette to converse about food. But Bengalis know the next best thing to eating is to talk about food.

As I was biking through a village bazaar, curious men stopped me to learn who I am and what is my purpose. Dozens clustered around us to observe me answering the interrogators. Suddenly, a stark naked crazy man broke through the crowd and demanded coins from me. I did him one better and invited Shiraj to lunch. After he had eaten his full, I handed Shiraj a cup of lemon tea, the way gentlemen end their meals. As they observed respect being shown to the mad one, the crowd became thoughtful.

Hakim suffered from dysentery, swollen limbs, and thin blood. He was placed in the hospital's isolation ward: broken windows, many mosquitoes, no light and no companions. I had to leave town for three days, and on my return I found him delirious and lying in his own filth. With my bare right hand I tried to feed him, conveying soft rice soaked in soup to his bearded mouth. How slowly he chewed; how difficult it was to swallow. Probably he did not even want the food but accepted it as a way of keeping someone at his side for a while.

To celebrate an anniversary I requested a widow, begging in the bazaar, to dine with me. Jabeda was flabbergasted by the offer, as were the numerous men who observed me ushering her inside the eatery. We sat across from each other but did not converse. Jabeda's eyes were on her dish. She relished every mouthful of steaming rice covered with spicy goat meat curry. Afterward, I fetched for her a wad of betel nut and leaf, the final course in any Bengali celebration. The meal apparently made her day, and surely made mine.

The home of Isa Khan, Bengali warrior of four centuries ago, is an impressive building, even though now it is a crumbling masterpiece. Amindat, a descendent of the warrior, lives in a humble house behind the historic one. He ordered that a heavy wooden chair resembling a throne be set out for me so that we could cement our friendship over cups of milk-tea. We sipped leisurely while he spoke with pride of his famous forebear.

The first time I met Alameen he was in his mother's arms. The three-year-old's sadly undernourished body was offset by a satisfied smile on his face. A biscuit in his hand was the cause of his joy. Shy and a bit scared when he saw me, he hesitated. Then, remembering one of the earliest lessons he had learned, he extended his arm, offering the precious biscuit to a stranger. Kids here learn early in life to share.

I was sitting alone in the Togetherness Restaurant minding my own business and dunking unleavened bread into split-pea soup. Three nicely dressed troublemakers interrupted. "I will kill you," the leader told me. Well, at least they don't ignore me.

It has become dangerous for me to go around town. Almost everywhere I wander friendly persons call out "Bob Brother!" as a greeting. The danger is that I rather like to hear it. Especially during my daily food shopping excursion to purchase potatoes, spinach, bananas, and an egg do I recall a warning aimed at those who love being greeted in the marketplace.

Friday is the day of the Muslims' weekly prayer assembly. It is my custom to invite for the noonday meal some person who cannot repay me. Blind Elim and his child guide accepted my invitation, and how they did delight in rice with fish curry! Afterward, the faith-filled Muslim prayed aloud to Allah in gratitude for the meal. He included me as a footnote in his prayer, but the main target was Allah. Elim knows Who gave growth to the food, Who enables digestion, and Who inspired me to invite him. To the Almighty, therefore, belong all praise and thanks. I think you'll agree that's not a bad theology.

Here's hoping that you, too, are sometimes able to enjoy sharing food with friends.

This Life Is a Parable of the Next

October 31, 1988
Kishoreganj

This year I dare not refrain from writing about the floods. "Tell your people what kind of a place this is we're living in," Bangladeshis urge me. This, therefore, is the first time I've ever written to you precisely as directed by the people.

Beginning in August, waters originating in the Himalaya mountains north of Bangladesh rushed into this deltaic plain on their way south to the Bay of Bengal. Those waters, augmented by our normal monsoon rainfall, flooded three-quarters of the nation. Practically speaking, Bangladesh was inundated.

Some of the stunned flood victims were welcomed into the already crowded huts of relatives. The majority, however, sought refuge in schools, *madrasas* (Islamic seminaries), and other public buildings. Conservative estimates claimed twenty million internal refugees. This agricultural country exactly the same size as the state of Iowa—but having a population density forty times that of Iowa—suddenly had to squeeze in an influx of anxious evacuees.

Had it been a flood of just a few days' duration, Bengali endurance and appetite for life could have made light of the instant sea in which they found themselves. Laughter and a song would have vanquished temporary inconvenience and loss. But the flood waters stayed.

Nor was it solely a matter of high water. In some areas—as in Kishoreganj District where I live—the entire eastern portion is under water for half of every year. They are accustomed to floods. The agents of destruction in our area were waves whipped up by strong winds. Waves pounded flimsy houses, which collapsed, disintegrated, and disappeared, like cubes of sugar splashed by coffee.

What were some of the peoples' first thoughts? "I am a day laborer, and now there is no work. Where will I get some money to buy rice or wheat flour to feed my children?" "My children are so lively; I have to keep close watch that they do not fall into the water and drown." "Almost all the village tube wells are submerged. Where will we find clean drinking water?" (In fact, more persons have died from diarrhea and other dirty-water diseases after the flood receded than from drowning during the flood.) "How can I cook a meal without dry firewood?" "Even where we sleep it is wet."

Perhaps the worst news concerns the future. A United Nations' report warns us that, henceforth, disastrous floods will be unstoppable annual events for Bangladesh. From now on, deforestation and soil erosion in Nepal will cause rain and silt to burst unchecked into Bangladesh. Even if a huge effort were being made within Bangladesh to faithfully dredge thousands of canals and rivers, there is no assurance that this nation could handle the excess

water invading us from Nepal by way of India. Flood control in Bangladesh is a clear illustration of international interdependence and the absolute necessity for cooperation among three nations to prevent the pulverization of one.

Are there any bright notes in all this? I shall mention one. In this catastrophe—as in others since 1970, that is, cyclone, tidal wave, war, famine—the people's Islamic faith has served them well. They perceive Allah's presence and power in these happenings. As I am a Christian missioner, it is not my intention to be an apologist for Islam. I began by telling you of the most severe flood in the history of the Indian subcontinent, and end by speaking of God-centered people. In truth, the flood victims are saved from despair only by their faith. And, as a respectful Christian witness of their lives, I rejoice to add: I am confident that the Islamic faith that saves them in this life will do no less in the life to come. This life is a parable of the next.

Postscript: We have not yet had a serious earthquake, but from time to time small ones shake us. Recently, at dawn, all was still and silent. Suddenly, a tremor awoke the neighborhood. Within seconds people from houses on every side of mine were outdoors, lifting voices and arms toward heaven, imploring Allah to help. Unrehearsed, they called on The Almighty, The Merciful One, from the depths of their hearts. It was like participating in a huge, open-air charismatic prayer meeting. In Bangladesh when the earth moves, the first thing detonated is the faith.

Look After Orphans and Widows in Their Distress

October 31, 1989
Netrakona

During the past fourteen years I've been privileged to live among the Muslims of Bangladesh. Occasionally I hear from Christian friends abroad that they are puzzled by my high regard for Islam and disappointed by my failure to convert Muslims. I offer the following interview in explanation:

Inquirer: What is a missioner?

Missioner: A missioner is a Christian sent to bring the Good News to persons afar.

Inquirer: What is this Good News?

Missioner: The Good News is the fact that God loves us all unconditionally and infinitely and that the way for all of us (that is, Christians, Muslims, Hindus, and others) to be happy in this life is to imitate God's way of loving: Jesus.

Inquirer: How does a missioner convey that fact to people?

Missioner: It depends on who the people are and what is their history. In Bangladesh, for example, 85 percent of the population is Muslim and 14 percent is Hindu. Both groups have strong, positive ideas about Jesus. They have learned of him and love him from their own Islamic and Hindu teachers.

Inquirer: In such a place what remains for a missioner to do?

Missioner: The hard part remains: a missioner can attempt to demonstrate the Good News by following Jesus 24 hours a day. By his friendly dealings with all persons, his cheerful service to the neediest and by his readiness to explain to the many Muslims who question "Why do you live this way?" a missioner can illustrate the Good News.

Inquirer: What difference does the people's history make?

Missioner: Plenty. Muslim Bengalis understand that for nearly two hundred years Englishmen (the term is synonymous in the Bengali mind with white-skinned Christians) subjugated and exploited their forefathers and their country. Colonialism is still a sore memory. They suspect that missioners' intentions toward them are selfish, a logical extension of colonialism, one more attempt to become their overlords. Bengali Muslims do not trust missioners.

Inquirer: So, it would be impossible to convert Bengali Muslims to Christianity?

Missioner: Quite the contrary. Educated middle-class young men have approached me to say, "I will become a Christian if you will give me a loan," or "if you will put me through college," or "if you will send me to your country." They would use their "conversion" as a commodity to be bartered for material benefits that I must provide.

Inquirer: Jesus told his apostles, "Go and preach the Gospel. He who believes and is baptized will be saved; but he who does not believe will be condemned." Are you an apostle, or not?

Missioner: I try to be a missioner for this age. I appreciate the teaching of Vatican Council II: "God does not deny the help necessary for salvation to anyone who strives to live a good life." That instruction corresponds with my experience of these deprived, often distressed, but good people. I do not fear for their damnation. Frequently I ask myself: How can I best evangelize and help these people? The answers that come: Spend yourself (Matt 20:28). Serve (John 13:15). Go and heal (Acts 10:38); look after orphans and widows in their distress (James 1:27).

Inquirer: Does your bishop support this way of evangelizing?

Missioner: The letter of assignment I have from Bishop Francis states five priority works for me: "Live among the poor as a brother to them. Serve the sick so that they may live. Show the respect that our Christian religion has for Islam and Hinduism. Explain to those who inquire about the reason for your lifestyle and good works. Contact the Christians in the area (a scattered few) and encourage them to lead good lives."

Inquirer: Did the bishop also advise you to live in this hut?

Missioner: Another great man from this subcontinent, Mahatma Gandhi, recommended it. His counsel to all persons who would evangelize in this culture: A life of service and uttermost simplicity is the best preaching.

Inquirer: How effective is the apostolate of witness and service as a way for revealing to Muslims the Jesus of Christianity?

Missioner: Islam is the state religion of Bangladesh, so the following example is not going to happen. But just imagine that a law were to be passed by the government

urging missioners to preach Christian faith openly. Even then I would choose to continue as at present. In other words, I am convinced that by striving to live among Muslims as a Christian brother, Muslims learn more about Christian faith than they could learn by hearing me preach about that faith.

Inquirer: Is it not probable that your witness will ultimately lead some sincere Muslims to embrace Christian faith and join the church?

Missioner: I have no idea, nor is that my aim. My aim is simply to live as Jesus lived and thereby build trust and friendship between followers of Jesus and followers of the Prophet Muhammad. The next step in our pilgrimage together will be up to God. I cannot predict it. But I have a hunch that what God will do for Christians and Muslims when they become open to one another will surprise and delight us all.

Trust and Friendship: Heart of Dialogue

October 31, 1990
Netrakona

Here is a thought question for you. Imagine this: You are a foreign Christian missionary living in a country where Islam is the state religion and a majority of the people are materially quite poor. Most of the people, especially the educated ones, have feelings of resentment toward white Christian foreigners because of a history of two hundred years under colonial rule, which ended in 1947. Many of the local Islamic religious leaders suspect you are a preacher, that you despise Islam, and that your goal is the conversion of Muslims to Christianity. What, then, is your mission approach to these people? What do you do among them?

Here is how I answer that. I try to be a Christian brother to Muslims. Thus, I dwell in a crowded, completely Muslim neighborhood and seek ways to help the seriously sick throughout a district having two million people. I try to make signs of friendship clearly and consistently and to explain them often: "I am your Christian brother. I am a missioner, that is, a servant of all God's people. Jesus went about doing good and healing because of his love for others. I follow Jesus. I wish to help the widow, the orphan, and the needy. Your religion and mine both teach that those who serve the poor serve Allah. I respect your Islamic faith. It is good. So is my Christian faith good. You fulfill your faith; I'll fulfill mine. We shall meet again in Paradise."

Islam, the religion of 85 percent, and Hinduism, the religion of 14 percent, help these good people, give them guidance and comfort, and move them to practice virtue. This is not the place or time for Christians to press ahead with missionary themes from the past, for example, Christianity is best; other religions and their rites are false or silly; conversion to Christianity is the only path to salvation. The church encourages in us a new attitude toward other faiths. We have this direction for our relationship with Muslims: "Although in the course of the centuries many quarrels and hostilities have arisen between Christians and Muslims, this most sacred Synod urges all to forget the past and to strive sincerely for mutual understanding. On behalf of all humankind, let Christians and Muslims make common cause of safeguarding and fostering social justice, moral values, peace, and freedom" (*Nostra Aetate* 3).

This, then, is a time for openness toward Muslims, respect for their beliefs, recognition of the spiritual fruits their faith yields for them, and determined Christian initiatives that aim to put cooperation where competition has been. Because a missioner understands and loves his own faith he is keen to demonstrate appreciation and respect for other faiths. Today's missioner pioneers respect for other faiths.

How is it possible for a Christian missioner to respect other faiths? First of all, I was brought up to respect others' faiths. I grew up in a town having a small Catholic population, a huge majority of Protestants, and a few Jewish families. I could see that almost all were good, decent folks. My parents respected them all, befriended many of them, and tolerated the few bad eggs. The biggest surprise of my first ten years came one day when a Protestant playmate confided to our little group that Catholics cannot be eternally saved. It was the most jolting remark I had ever heard. I asked myself: "How can this bright pal of mine think such a dumb thought?" I knew I'd never be damned for professing my kind of faith in God. I sensed that judging the faith of others is ridiculous. I still feel that way.

"What will I receive if I become a Christian?" is a question Muslims put to me. The majority of the inquirers are merely displaying their contempt for the alleged willingness of some missioners to tempt the poor and purchase their conversion. Although the missioners who strive to make converts are not principally Catholics, we Catholic missioners share their notorious reputation by association. Muslims' deeply negative perception of all missioners will perdure for as long as some missioners continue to stress the conversion of Muslims as the goal of mission in Bangladesh. Fifteen years of living closely with Muslims teaches me that they are profoundly suspicious that missioners do good to the poor solely in order to convert them to Christianity. Sad to say, there is some basis in fact—both historical and current—for that perception. The most effective remedy for this jaundiced Muslim view is, in my experience, for the missioner to forswear conversion as the purpose of mission. The church is pleading for Christians and Muslims to work together. But we and they can only work together enduringly with persons we trust. Muslims cannot trust missioners among them unless the missioners plainly exclude the intention to make converts.

Recently, a missioner asked this question about the future of Christian mission among the nations: "If conversion is no longer the primary focus of missioners, then is not the work of mission finished?" Surely, I believe, it is not finished. The task of mission continues, but with a fresh focus. The Asian bishops speak knowledgeably about the need for the church to create a spirit of harmony among all religions and people in Asia.

I think the day is coming soon when the primary responsibility laid on missioners in countries such as

Bangladesh will be to build trust and friendship with persons of other faiths. Who else but missioners can be expected to initiate and exemplify this new attitude of the church—that is, the spirit of fraternal cooperation toward Muslims, Hindus, and others? In Bangladesh, missioners are obviously the first Christians who must demonstrate it. Muslims and others regard missioners as the official representatives of the Christian religion. They conclude that as the missioners behave, so their faith teaches. Thus, if missioners are concerned with efforts to convert Muslims, it means that the Christian religion devalues the faith that Muslims love, and is by dialogue merely trying to trick and transfer believing Muslims into the "foreign" religion. But if the alleged new openness of Christians toward Muslims is sincere, then Muslims will be able to judge the truth of that claim by observing the missioners' lives and dealings with Muslims.

Among the 110 millions of Bangladeshis are 300,000 Christians. These good folks also need proof that the church has a new attitude toward Muslims. If Christians do not see that attitude enfleshed in their own missioners, then where can they find it?

Bangladeshi Christians ask me: "What results do you have to show for years of living among Muslims?" I reply "Nothing tangible," because there is no physical memorial of this work—no schools started, parishes established, or cooperatives begun. However, I do seem to have a lot of Muslim friends and well-wishers, most of whom were initially suspicious of "the missionary." Later, they were surprised by his love for the poor and respect for their faith. These Muslims have ended up speaking enthusiastically about the missioner's life and the service he gives without any expectation of reward. Trust and friendship are growing. Who could ask for anything more?

Responding to an Emergency

October 31, 1991
Netrakona

The cyclone and tidal wave that smashed through the Bay of Bengal several months ago transpired 160 miles south of my Netrakona home. Thus I joined a relief team formed by Caritas Bangladesh to assist the people of Sandwip.

Sandwip is an island along the southeastern coast of Bangladesh in the Chittagong District, 15 sq. miles in area, lying barely above sea level. High tides menace the island, depending on the strength of the wind. Nevertheless, 30,000 persons—farmers and fisher folk, mostly, Muslims and Hindus—all brave the dangerous environment and trust in the Merciful One to save them from harm. Local people claim 36 cyclones have slammed across the island during the past 31 years. This year, the cyclone's velocity was higher than ever: 145 miles per hour. Thus, water at high tide during the terrible night of April 29-30 was whipped up into waves that reached 20 feet in height. Between 11 p.m. and 4 a.m. people clung to tree tops or, if lucky, found safety atop buildings or in the concrete storm shelters. Some parents tied their children high up on the trunks of coconut trees only to discover afterward they had failed to tie them high enough. Stories abound that make me feel I have not yet really been tested.

From this single island 6,200 deaths were accounted for. Yet, during 21 days on Sandwip I saw no grieving among the stunned survivors.

Sanitation and hygiene had been rendered abysmal by the cyclone and tidal surge. As predicted, a cholera epidemic broke out. More than 1,700 new cases of diarrhea were being reported daily. The relief team's health contingent—Sister Judy Walter and myself—decided that the best way to help would be to offer intravenous cholera fluid to doctors in eighteen health centers throughout the island. Interaction with Bengali health personnel who were wearing themselves down for their people edified us. We were grateful to find bicycles for rent available

locally without which our coverage of the entire island would have been impossible.

Feelings of compassion among the 35 relief team members were also tinged with regret. Numerous volunteers cited examples of selfishness among the storm victims which distressed them. I, too, was troubled when told in village Sultanpur that only a hundred families remained in Pach Baria, the next village. I should not worry about so few persons, they implied: I should concern myself with Sultanpur. Yet, I know that the people who made that thoughtless suggestion are, in fact, basically good people. For I see no bitterness in them. If they were not human beings closely attuned to the Divine they would be bitter. They had just lost family members, homes, livestock, crops, nets, and belongings. They realize it may well happen again. In circumstances such as they live in I could only hope to be as free from bitterness as these good people are. That is not to say these temporarily crushed people are saints. The truth is they are much like us, although their faith in the Creator has been tried and tempered by violent deprivation more frequently than has ours.

One day, after bicycling along eight miles of hilariously muddy roads, I sloshed through a congested, severely battered village. The people's hospitality moved me. Later, as I cycled back to our relief camp, I beheld a scene of happy contentment. In front of his demolished home and several uprooted trees a bare-chested grandfather hugged his infant grandson. I stopped, enchanted. What's his name? I asked. Grandpa thought hard but could not recall it. I reached for the little fellow: he came to me willingly, fascinated by my spectacles. I was laying a kiss on his cheek at the very moment his older brothers excitedly ran to my side with the information I had requested: "His name is Saddam Hossain!"

Gigantic surges of the agitated sea obliterated 11.5 miles of embankment that had been built painstakingly, by hand labor, to repel just such an invasion. Rebuilding and repairing forty miles of embankment is the islanders' most pressing current task.

A sympathetic person might ask: "Why don't the people of Sandwip abandon that perilous place?" The answer: "Please do suggest another spot to them." People do not stay on Sandwip because they welcome the challenge. There simply is no more unoccupied space in Bangladesh.

Compassionate Stranger

October 31, 1992
Jamalpur

Nowadays, I live in a kitchen. Jabeda, the wife of Firoz and mother of their eleven children, rented the family's cooking shed to me three months ago on the day I arrived in Jamalpur town to begin missioning in a new area. On that first day, I searched for a hut to rent but received, instead, numerous refusals. No Muslim family having girls will easily agree to accept a single male into their compound. Then, inexplicably, Allah inspired Jabeda to take a chance on the foreign Christian. "You don't want a place that simple, do you?" she asked me incredulously, while pointing to her kitchen hut. Indeed, I did. At that moment I was gratefully aware that God was intervening through a Muslim woman to relieve my anxiety.

No sooner had I taken possession of the cooking shed than I had to rush off to hardware stores to buy basic kitchen equipment and utensils. The first item prepared on my new kerosene stove was a gallon of boiled water. Folks here do not boil the water they drink. Children gawked as I gulped the barely cooled fluid. Even greater surprises are in store for them, and for me, as we mutually observe one another.

The cooking shed stands four yards away from the family's house. It measures almost eight feet by ten, has a bamboo roof, and incomplete walls made mostly of bamboo and partially of rusty tin. There is no ceiling for trapping heat beneath the roof. The floor is earthen and not level. Into it two clay stoves are sunk, remnants of the years when Jabeda and her seven daughters cooked rice and curry to feed a family of thirteen.

Food preparation requires more time than I want to give it, but the alternative is to eat inexpensive, delicious, peppery hot Bengali cuisine in local restaurants until, inevitably, a dysenteric explosion would strike me down. Each day I spend half an hour at the bazaar picking out vegetables for supper, a duck's egg for breakfast, and rice with lentils for lunch. Cleaning the food takes another twenty minutes. Cooking all three meals takes less than an hour, total time, during which I read. The family has their own tube well, which is convenient, and a latrine more private than ones I've gotten used to. Surrounding the family's compound is a fence constructed of jute sticks: it has a single, narrow exit through which I squeeze my bicycle

Firoz and Jabeda expect one hundred takas per month for allowing me to share the family compound. Thus, rent is less than U.S. 9 cents per day. Their twin teenaged daughters, Chaya and Maya (the names mean Shade and Affection), take down my drying clothes if it rains while I am away, a kindness for which there is no charge. Rain frequently penetrates the roof and dampens the hut.

Occasionally, on days when I am away, one of the twins enters to spread fresh mud mixed with rice bran on the floor. It is the Muslim Bengalis' way to keep a house neat. There is no way to attach a lock to the bamboo door, and even if it were lockable, any determined person could enter through twenty square feet of open space above the walls. Thus, even though my door is not always open, the house always is.

Days begin at 4 a.m. in prayer followed by Mass. Then I shave and eat breakfast. The remainder of the day is a stew of spicy activities. By bicycle I ride to many villages to meet seriously sick persons. Conversations are frequent and arguments (a form of entertainment in Bangladesh) occasional. I haggle over food prices in the bazaar and visit the children's ward at the government hospital to bless Muslim and Hindu tots. In every corner of the district women regard warily the recently arrived foreign missionary who offers concern and assistance to their ailing loved ones. It will take time to build trust with them. Men express astonishment when they see an old man on a battered bike traveling great distances at high speed. They want to know what I get out of such strenuous labor. I explain to them my thoughts about Allah and the part that Jesus plays in my life. Every late afternoon beside the neighborhood mosque I wash clothes and bathe in a large fish tank. While I pound sudsy laundry on a rock, curious youths sit on the bank and shoot questions at me. By nightfall, the hut is cooler. It is not connected to electric current, so my sight and mind grow dim by 9 p.m. or earlier. Sleep comes quickly on a mat spread on a wooden cot.

Jamalpur, the town in which I've settled, is a rail junction located on the Brahamaputra River. The municipality has 101,000 people. The district of Jamalpur which surrounds it has a population of less than two million. In the town are a score of mosques and three cinema halls. An odd feature about the main street of the town is that it changes names ten times within 1.5 miles. Door-to-door research at thirty stores informs me there is not a single wooden clothespin for sale, anywhere.

My periodic transfers from one district town to another are in imitation of Jesus' approach to mission. Jesus, the compassionate stranger, moved from area to area and in every place paid special attention to the hopelessly infirm and to sick ones who had no relatives or friends to assist them. The crowds who witnessed Jesus's acts were gripped by his compassion, and not exclusively by his cures. Bengali Muslims are no less astounded to receive compassion from a stranger.

You Will Never Lose Anything While Living among Us

October 31, 1993
Jamalpur

After I had lived for ten weeks in a rented cooking shed, Nizam, a cart-puller, and Golenor, his versatile wife, offered me their entire, wee garden space in which to build the hut of my dreams. I snatched at the chance to move to their neighborhood: poorer, more crowded, and replete with Bengali children who make me smile.

At the beginning of our construction work Nizam measured seven hands (10.5 feet) on a fifteen-foot-long bamboo pole, laid the pole on the ground as a guide, and commenced digging post holes in the soft earth at 2.5 foot intervals. I scooped out the loosened earth with my hands and thanked God for the privilege of working closely with persons who know fifty times more than I about erecting a house.

Along with Nizam and his brother Quddus, Golenor skillfully split shafts of bamboo into thin, flat pieces. Then they manufactured walls that "breathe." One variety of bamboo (called *Sherpur*) was used to weave the four walls. Another, thicker variety (*Rail*) was used for the roof. While we men were resting, Golenor dug up potatoes, which would otherwise soon push up through my floor. "See how we are all working on your house?" she teased me in a voice that all the neighbors could hear. "It is because of our *mahabbat* (love). We are poor," she continued, "but you will never lose anything while living among us." That touched me. They are right to give pride of place to virtues—for example honesty and the protection of a neighbor's goods from theft—and not to waste time or energy on mere fancy housing.

The skeleton of thick bamboo stems was lashed together with ropes. Nary a nail was used. The walls were raised and attached by baling wire to sixteen posts. Then, the roof was fitted snugly onto the upper framework. Not far away we located some earth for sale and used it to raise the floor a few inches above the level that water reaches during the rainy season. As our task concluded, strong wires were slung over both ends of the roof and anchored

firmly in the ground on both sides of the hut. Those wires, God willing, will keep the roof from flying away during storms. Golenor added the final touch by hacking a hole into the eastern wall, facing the breeze. Then, with a scrap of tin she fashioned a shutter for the exclusive window.

On the third day, our work was finished. I'd become the satisfied owner of a home eighty square feet in area for the cost of 1,880 takas (i.e., nearly fifty dollars). Nizam proclaimed a welcome from the whole family: "You can stay 200 years with us." Quddus pledged that if I die while living among them, he will personally carry me to the Islamic cemetery. I insisted, rather, to be placed beside the new house they had built for me. "That is better!" enthused Nizam, "for it makes no difference at all where the body goes. The soul goes to Allah!"

According to the Bengali custom, I bought sweets to felicitate my neighbors on the occasion of building a new house in their midst. When I carried the three one-kilo-gram boxes home from the sweets shop Golenor warned me to hide the stuff. "Don't show the children," she said seriously. With a smile she added: "They will eat every-thing you've got in the boxes and then start eating you!" She was kidding, I thought. But then Nizam informed me that he would be the distributor of the sweets—and not I—but not before it got sufficiently dark outside. After dark the kids would be in their homes and not prowl-ing around. Surely there cannot be so many children in this small neighborhood, I protested. "*Haaaayyy* Brother! There are no less than two hundred kids within one hun-dred yards of this house!" Nizam set me straight. Later, Nizam walked door to door in the dark bearing a pan, in which were forty pieces of *rasshagolla* (syrupy, super sweet balls made of sugar and cream). I accompanied him from behind and could only laugh as adults let him plop the sticky, ping-pong-sized balls into their bare right hands. By accepting them they accepted their new neighbor.

A proverb claims that Bengalis live for their children. Eight of these loved ones live in three of the huts facing mine. In one hut: Ratna, age twelve years, because of whose hip injury I first got to know the family, is the oldest child and knows how to give commands. Yusuf (that's Joseph), nine, enjoys streaking through the neighborhood clothed in nothing but mud. Rena, six, their singing, smiling sister, has already learned to conceal hunger with cheerfulness. In another hut: Kakuli, nine, a dark beauty, is usually elsewhere whenever her mother needs her. Sheuli, seven, protests every order and demands to know, "Why should I?" Rubel, two, is a youngest child and only son, and therefore the dearest extended family member. In the last hut: Labhlu, ten, needs to be prodded to study because his mind is quicker than other kids his age. Resma, eight, his sister, warmed to me slowly, but now follows me whenever I go to the tube well, to take delight in the spectacle of my bath.

It did not occur to me until I'd been living with them for a month that this family and those surrounding us are Shandars, that is, gypsies. Perhaps, by association with them, I'm one, too.

Mahatma Gandhi empathized with the feelings of Bengali Muslims. He urged Christian missionaries to enter into their mentality by lives of "uttermost simplicity." My excellent companions on the path of simplicity and downward mobility are day laborers and cart pullers, their homemaking wives, and irrepressible children. By attaching myself to them I seek to put on their minds. The pursuit of a Bengali Muslim mentality, like the effort to put on the mind of Christ, has something to do with solving the problem of the poor, but even more to do with sharing their condition.

Golenor: A Builder of Peace

October 31, 1994
Jamalpur

Although she is a mere two years older than I, Golenor treats me as her son. This good mother keeps an eye on my hut while I am out, and makes repairs in the earthen floor and bamboo walls and roof when needs arise. She is solicitous for my welfare, takes practical steps to make my home life smooth, and offers timely suggestions. She is a builder of peace.

One day, Nizam brought home a jackfruit to treat the entire family. There was no question about who would open the treasure for the expectant children and adults. While seventeen persons crowded around to watch, Golenor ripped apart the huge, rough fruit with her bare hands. Expertly she dissected the fleshy parts from their dense, sticky surroundings. I do not know of any task this woman puts her hands to that she does not do well. She easily fits the biblical description of a "noble woman"— even though her holy book is the Quran. Her husband, Nizam, is blessed by Golenor. In fact, he is twice blessed because his younger wife, Rabia, is a good person, too.

Although Golenor and Rabia had both been complaining of fever and aches, they set aside their feelings one day to dig a large hole in the ground for our new outhouse. Golenor stood inside the hole, digging, and passed up the loosened earth to Rabia for her to dispose. They did not eat all day long while accomplishing the job. They had no money to employ men for the task. After the hole had reached six feet, Golenor climbed out. Together they removed the cement platform from the old toilet, placed it over the freshly dug hole, and sealed the former pit with earth. Then, they built flimsy walls from jute sticks to enclose the house. Golenor invited me to view the result of their sweat-soaked effort. Most people in Bangladesh do not draw attention to their outhouses, but these two women were understandably proud of what their hands had wrought.

One evening, Golenor brought to me a plateful of rice and fish. I had begged her not to do it, but she would not listen. It had been so long a time since the family had enjoyed a large fish that they wished to share their joy. Golenor knows, of course, that no person actually wants to be excluded from eating steaming white rice with a hunk of salty fried fish on the side. It is delightful! However, I have never lived with Bengalis who eat fish as seldom as does this family. They love fish, naturally; all Bengalis do.

But large fish are expensive and, therefore, not often seen on the plates of the poor. Their generosity brings to mind an interesting comparison. This Muslim family procures a rare large fish, so they force me to partake of it. On the other hand, this Christian missioner infrequently gets hold of a chocolate bar, and I do not even announce it.

Service to seriously sick and disabled persons who are too poor to even think of going for treatment continues to be my contribution to Bangladesh. What differentiates this service from the help offered by other concerned persons is the emphasis on outreach. That is, I go in search of persons who need a brother to care about their broken health. I do not wait in my hut for people to look me up. This outreach aspect requires physical labor, bicycling in particular, the kind of effort that highly educated persons in this culture are not expected to exert. It is regarded by many as demeaning to sweat for others. On the contrary, I imagine that sweat is a symbol of love.

The five huts in our compound are so hot inside that after dark we sit outside in a circle fanning ourselves. One evening, Nozrul (Golenor's son-in-law), requested me to give him my hand fan. "Are you quite warm?" I inquired. Hamida heard our exchange from where she was cooking, and chimed in with an explanation for me. "Nozrul doesn't want the fan for himself. He wants to fan you! Everybody looks for an opportunity to serve you because you are always serving everyone else."

Hamida (Golenor's daughter-in-law) frequently explains things for Nozrul … or to him. One evening, Nozrul magnanimously extolled Christians. How good Christian customs are, he explained, and how similar are our two faiths! Hamida, younger than he (and a woman, besides), did not care for the exaggerated attention he was heaping on the Prophet Jesus. She reminded Nozrul curtly that Muhammad is the Last Prophet. A verbal duel was in the offing until Hamida put a stop to it. She is a woman of short temper, but also has redeeming common sense.

One of the most enthusiastically friendly professional persons I know in Jamalpur is a college professor. Early one morning as he was returning home from the bazaar with a bagful of vegetables he spied me in a barber shop. He wanted to hear about America. "I know of your Columbus and Clinton, but I want to know something about the great Americans who came between them." I had other work to do, so I excused myself, but I pledged to him that I would try to think of some outstanding persons. The professor teaches history, so this is my chance to help him get it straight. I shall jot down eight or ten names for him—mostly women's. My present living environment is influencing me.

From Rome the Congregation for Institutes of Consecrated Life and Societies of Apostolic Life recently published a document in which it is stated that "a religious man or woman living alone must be an extremely rare exception." The authors are anxious, apparently, about religious or members of apostolic societies who are so immersed in the lives of the people that there is little opportunity for prayer and socializing with members of their own religious families. I do believe that if the authors of that document were to accompany me here they would discover that a missioner can also belong to another community—an Islamic one, that it is advantageous for the

cause of peace that some missioner in Islamic Bangladesh
dwell with Muslims, and that bonds with other Maryknollers in Bangladesh remain strong because of our common vision, mutual concern, and a monthly retreat day
together. To restrict a missioner in Bangladesh to living
and socializing principally within a small religious community would be, it seems to me, to cautiously step back
from engagement with Christ in the Islamic world.

Periodically I make time to visit the towns where I previously lived. Thus did I journey to Netrakona to spend
five exhilarating, encouraging hours. The town had nearly
recovered from its most recent flood. Lots of folks greeted
me as I came into town by rickshaw from the bus station,
and later as I rode a bicycle loaned to me by a friend. I had
not intended to assist sick persons during such a short stay,
but I ended up doing so because people needed help. In
my old neighborhood, Islampur, I shook scores of hands,
little and big, and held a couple of the newborn. Finally,
I ate dinner with Samsu Miah and his wife, Putul, a person who has not always been keen on me. As I took the
bus away from the town, I questioned myself. What more
could I want from life than that which is given: the conviction that God's purpose for me is being fulfilled, friends
who are glad to see me, and limitless opportunities to be
useful to others? I owe God an eternity of thanks.

Suspicion . . . Trust . . . and Affection

October 31, 1995
Sherpur

Stability in one place is advantageous for most professions. Yet, contrasted with teachers, pastors, lawyers, doctors, monks, and others, I often shift from one location to another. There is good reason, I think, for my periodic moves from familiar to unknown places.

When, in 1986, after having lived for nine years in Tangail District I departed for Kishoreganj District, I had no idea how long God would inspire me to remain in the newly chosen area. Then, after spending a mere two years in the new town, I understood that one additional year would suffice. I could see that the sign I had come to make was becoming widely accepted and respected—although there were some persons who from the first until the final day of my stay yearned for me to be gone. Roughly speaking, the pattern that emerged in Kishoreganj has been repeated in Netrakona, and again, most recently, in Jamalpur. Three years of residence in each district town, and frequent bicycle journeys to myriad villages of the district surrounding the town, is sufficient duration to offer testimony of Christian—that is, radically unselfish—love.

In every one of the towns where I have lived alone among Muslims each passing year has been marked by a characteristic attitude of the local people toward me.

Broadly speaking, the first year is distinguished by suspicion. Upon learning that I am a Christian missionary Muslims easily suspect that my motive for coming among them is harmful, that is, to convert them from Islam—the religion of their birth, which binds them to a community in which they feel secure. Those who are not threatened by my presence are at least mystified by it. Why, they wonder, would anyone choose to live in a bamboo hut among persons with whom he is totally unacquainted, having no other program than service to sick and disabled persons? Why would a foreigner offer service in such an inefficient way—using a bicycle instead of a motorcycle for travels, and using kerosene instead of electricity at home? They want to know how my parents, siblings, and other relatives feel about my attending to the needs of persons outside our family. I explain to Muslims that I am their Brother Bob and that Allah inspires me to dwell among them and do among them as Jesus did. Christian parents, I explain, crave to have children who will dedicate themselves to God. Unselfish families believe that the Most Generous One blesses them.

The second year is marked by a growth in trust. The poor whom I assist are the first to trust. They do not require much explanation about my identity and purpose. They quickly sense that I am for them and that my intention is wholly benevolent. When I go around on a bicycle searching for persons seriously in need of physical healing, they perceive an able-bodied old-timer who seems eager to toil for their well-being. I accompany them to hospitals; some I even carry there. Healthy persons—

especially those who are educated and members of the economic middle class—discuss among themselves the sight they see. They ask me, "What is in this for you?" Happiness now and an eternal reward, I reply. Faith-filled, pious Muslims approach and tell me: "Although Islam is the best religion, no Muslim would ever inconvenience himself for others the way you do." When Muslims observe no-strings-attached love, it smacks them with the force of personally experienced revelation. Apparently, my presence helps them to reflect.

During the third year I can sense an increase of their affection. By then, I am nearly everybody's "uncle," or, to fewer, "father," that is, *abba*. Adults acknowledge me in public places; children greet me cheerfully. Young men shout a friendly "Bob Brother!" and some of them, perhaps referring to my riding habits, hail me with a thunderous "Young man!" Curious men cease to interrogate me distrustfully and begin to question me calmly, as if to signal that they are no longer interested to prove that the claims of my Christian religion are false but, rather, they wish to understand better the reasons for my way of life and concern for the lives of neglected others. Mothers hand me their children to hug and to bless and, occasionally, to name. "Does your family not miss you?" adults inquire. "Who will bury and weep for you if you die in this faraway place?" I reply that my family has sent me to them, and that they pray to God and sacrifice financially so that I can continue to be useful to Muslims. As for death, I propose that nobody ever dies. Muslims, Hindus, Buddhists, and Christians—all shall live forever.

That, approximately, is the pattern that is duplicated every three years in a new location. There are, of course, persons who trust the missioner from the very start. For them, there is no first step: suspicion. On the other hand, there are some whose suspicion of missioners never ceases. They are stuck in their biases. However, as a practical rule, Muslims who observe the missioner living in the thick of their everyday lives are struck first by suspicion, then by trust, and finally by affection.

Thus have I concluded significant stays in four district towns. Nevertheless, my connection with every locality has not been terminated. In fact, it remains fresh through the periodic visits that I make. At least twice a year I return to Tangail and to Kishoreganj. I pay even more frequent visits to Netrakona and Jamalpur. The people in the four towns are accustomed to see me return. I have overheard surprised Muslims ask one another, "Why did he come back? Will he live here again?" Another replies correctly: "No. He simply wants to see his friends again." Over a period of time friendships have matured and horizons have expanded. Onlookers have become well-wishers as they grow accustomed to the notion that it is possible for a Christian to truly respect Muslims, light-skinned to be concerned for dark-skinned, and educated to cordially serve unlettered. The hostile term "missionary" is taking on new meaning.

A perceptive missioner once elucidated the purpose of this profession: "To be a missioner is to go where you are needed but not wanted, and to stay until you are wanted but not needed." My moving at intervals of three years is related to that insight.

Postscript: Have I received any surprises from all of this moving around? Yes, and one in particular. It seems to me that it has taken less time to gain my neighbors' trust every time I have transferred to a new district. I deduce that it is because I am aging. It is easier for Bengalis to trust older persons. If there is any other factor that accounts for the people's quicker acceptance of me as I progress from one town to another then only Allah knows it. All I know is that growing old has its apostolic advantages, and aging is not to be automatically deplored by an evangelizer.

I Am Indeed Their Brother

October 31, 1996
Sherpur

Bangladeshi Muslims hardly know what to think of me during my first year in a new town. They see me going around on a bicycle and have heard that I go long distances on it. Rumor has it that I am willing to help seriously afflicted persons and that I live in a hut. They know I am a foreigner by my complexion. It does not add up. For them, foreigners are those who have autos to drive and who are, in fact, usually driven here and there by their hired local drivers. Besides, foreigners live among themselves, generally in houses surrounded by walls. Thus, a missioner living among Muslims, for service to their disabled ones, arouses suspicion.

What does it mean to say they are suspicious of me? Recently, we passed the first-year anniversary of my coming to Sherpur town. Here is a brief review of the people's expressed perceptions of this newly arrived outsider. Five names have been given to me, more than others.

"He is a reporter." This is not said in admiration. Many Bangladeshis imagine that the country's international reputation is at least partly owed to foreign reporters who critically observe and tattle to the world about the nation's insufficiencies. It does not make them happy to be presented to the world as poor. Unfortunately, I have the unusual, but necessary, custom of carrying a ballpoint pen and scrap paper in my pocket at all times—mainly because my memory has leaks in it and I must stop to jot down the thoughts that occur to me whenever they strike, whether on the road or in the bazaar. The penchant to jot does not alleviate suspicion. Just the opposite. "What is he writing?" they want to know as they hasten to my side in the bazaar or surround my bike on the trail.

"He is a spy." This is a variation of the above-mentioned perception. Those who voice it are educated men who want everyone to know that they are aware of the spying profession and too sophisticated to be tricked by a foreign agent. This misidentification reaches my ears through third parties, for example, "They say you are a spy."

"He is a police agent." It is mostly children who declare this perception. For instance, they are playing on the village path or in the fields alongside when I travel through. Their young eyes balloon, jaws sag. Surrendering to the impulse to identify the passerby, one daringly blurts "Police!" These good people have a strong sense of control over village paths and public roads. A bicyclist journeying along "their" path, far from his own home, customarily rides slowly, that is, humbly. I, like a policeman, probably give them the impression of a person in authority, that is, unafraid. When they label me police it is no compliment, for police are feared. (The military, on the other hand, is trusted and respected. Bright young men eagerly join it. I am not compared with the soldiers.)

Incidentally, it would tickle me if someone would say, in recognition of frequent and strenuous bicycle trips, "He is an athlete." But I have not heard that during these

twenty-one years in Bangladesh. What I have heard from the bus drivers and conductors with whom I often cross paths is considerably less flattering: "He is a machine." That is what expending lots of energy gets for me during year one in Sherpur.

"He is a doctor." Anyone in this country who works for the cure of the sick is regarded as a doctor. No medical degree is required to win this designation. Involvement with the afflicted is everything. Doctors are respected. In fact, in the minds of villagers, it may be the most respected profession, on a par with teaching and much ahead of business. Still, people are unaccustomed to doctors who make house calls afar, and baffled by one who will pedal for hours to seek out a sufferer. Besides, they wonder what sort of doctor it is who is unashamed to arrive wearing sweat-soaked clothes. Hence, when they call me doctor suspicion remains.

"He is a missionary." There are some who, from the very beginning, suspect it. In their view, a missionary is even more harmful than a reporter or spy and more threatening than a police agent. Their concept of a missionary is so negative that they need re-education. They think it means a preacher whose sole purpose is to convert them to another religion. That is why I explicitly and unfailingly introduce myself as a missionary and then, always, explain its meaning in terms they had not associated with mission: follower, servant, helper, lover, brother.

A conspicuous feature of Bengalis—a characteristic that makes the missioner's life easier, it seems to me—is their unabashed curiosity. They inquire quite directly; they want to know what I have to say about myself. Thus, they often call for me to stop. "What are you doing here?" they ask without hesitation. I reply that I am a Christian missionary, a follower of Jesus, a servant of Allah. Allah's servant has concern for the sick or disabled who have no one else. The Compassionate One loves us all. Allah loves me and I love Allah. My involvement with those who suffer is an act of love for Allah. I am your brother. We can all be brothers and sisters if we want it.

Others there are who cannot overlook a defect in my

physical appearance. Again, it is mostly children who stare intently upon my missing tooth (a lateral incisor), point to it, and call my disfigurement to the attention of their cohorts. Occasionally they taunt "the guy with the missing tooth." They do not know that I own a false tooth attached to a partial denture, or that when I insert the denture I can scarcely pronounce their Bengali language. Thus, since 1975 I have refrained from using that mouthpiece. Like many missioners I know, I'd rather look funny than sound funny.

A salutary saying urges Christians: We must not only be good but, also, be perceived as good. After spending one year in Sherpur I am not yet generally perceived to be good. However, suspicions are melting. Perhaps, in a while, more persons will perceive me to be a missionary in the sense best suited for Christians living among Bangladeshi Muslims during the final years of the twentieth century. Meanwhile, even while they do not so perceive me, I am indeed their brother. As Jesus, my model in life, was mistaken for a glutton and drunkard. I should not let peoples' initial misperceptions derail me.

Postscript: Earlier this year Orbis Books published *Dialogue of Life*, which is my wee contribution to advancing respect among followers of all religions.

A Friend of the Poor

October 31, 1997
Sherpur

Two years have passed since I came to Sherpur, my present location. The initial suspicions of the people that my purpose among them may be harmful have given way, generally, to trust. Signs of their growing trust are these:

Every Wednesday when I return from having assisted the sick and disabled at the regional hospital, I arrive home just before dusk. Children are playing in the lane that leads to my bamboo dwelling. A hundred "Okay!'s" reverberate as they welcome me home. (That nickname, given me by the children, sticks. Thus, there are adults in the town who believe my name is not Bob, but Okay.) Sometimes the kids seize my hands and pull me home as if I could not otherwise complete the journey without their hearty assistance. They would not be so friendly unless their parents also approved of me. Children add gestures and sound to their elders' quiet acceptance of a newcomer.

Rehana suffers from diabetes. She is fourteen but looks to be forty. Treatment is available 25 miles away, the last ten miles of which are difficult. Seeing no other solution, I invited the shriveled teenager to sit on the carrier behind me as I bicycled cautiously through bamboo groves on rugged paths. Her parents agreed to our excursion because they had been assured by other villagers that my concern is genuine and not a ruse for taking advantage of their poverty or their daughter's defenselessness. At one

79

point in our journey the exhausted girl fell off, and as she groaned I also cried out: "Oh, no! Now you'll have a broken leg, besides." But Allah preserved Rehana. Then a few bumpy miles farther along, she fell a second time. I was sure that the law of averages had caught up with us. A broken arm would be small-enough punishment. But not a bone was broken, for nothing is impossible for God.

Men expect me, a foreigner, to play the big shot. It would not surprise them to perceive arrogance in someone such as I. Recently, a disabled fellow, having completed his X-ray, was unable to leave the X-ray room because he could not reach his shoes. I asked if he would allow me to help, assisted him in swinging his legs off the X-ray table, and wiggled the shoes onto his feet. He left the room praising me for an ordinary kindness. Extraordinary, however, in the viewpoint of a Bengali Muslim, for I had willingly touched his feet and shoes, contact with which Bengalis strive always to avoid. Meanwhile, the X-ray technician was so amazed by my humility (his view of it) that he gave my head a little squeeze.

Tired from bicycling, I turned in at 8:00 p.m. Under the mosquito net, with a hurricane lamp and reading materials, I reclined for night prayers. Afterward, while reading from a humor magazine, I felt myself drifting away. Before I could extinguish the lamp a familiar voice called to me. Banesa, a working widow, had come to visit. I protested that I was already in bed, but she wanted to talk, so out from under the net I came and slid open the flimsy door. We stood there to converse. She inquired about my health and I about hers. Banesa is an attractive thirty-year-old mother of two. Whenever we meet, I commend her for the constancy of her efforts to earn money. She wanted to tell me the good news that she had gotten a raise. Now she earns 50 takas ($1.15) plus three meals for every strenuous twelve-hour workday at a restaurant in the town. From that amount Banesa gives 40 takas daily to her mother to feed the children. She excused herself for getting me out of bed, complaining: "I never get off work until you are in bed!" When she departed, smiling, I blessed her and she blessed me ... a pretty good way to end our days.

As I poured off the excess water from my noonday meal two women approached the opened door. Captivated, they watched as steam from the pot flew into my face. I could tell from their dress and manner that they had not come to see me in order to speak about illness, as do many of the visitors to my hut. Setting aside the rice pot, I spread a cloth on the edge of the bed board and bid them enter to be seated. They are teachers at the local school, where four hundred pupils are handled in two shifts by five teachers. They had been visiting the neighborhood and took this occasion to see me at home. Their questions about good works and lifestyle followed; my answers satisfied them. I showed them a photo of my mother and father, vintage 1976. It helped the women to put me into a human perspective. The photograph implies that we are not so different: we all have parents. As they departed, Samsunahar and Nazma Begum expressed how much they like to see me serving the poor and living among them. Each one spoke the same sentiments in different words, reinforcing approval. Although the days before their visit had brimmed with tension because the owner of the plot on which my house stands would like to have it back, it is also true that during two years in Sherpur I have not heard more explicit support than that offered by the two encouraging women.

Wandering through a vacant government office building, I suddenly encountered a nicely suited gentleman on the verandah. "You are Brother Bob!" he informed me as he grasped me for a triple embrace. I could recall having seen the man before, but where or when baffled me. "I was a magistrate in Netrakona for five years," he reminded me. "When you lived there, you used to go to the provincial jail at Christmas time to give bars of soap to the prisoners. Do you remember that, Brother?" Surely, I did. Again he gripped my arm and began to pull me toward his office for a cup of tea. I begged to be excused. I was intent on meeting the very officer who could give me permission to visit the local prison on Christmas day. Unselfishly, my long-lost friend allowed me to pass. He likes to see concern for forgotten persons.

Whereas it could not have happened a year or two ago, now it happens that Muslim Bengalis make excuses for my mistakes. Recently, I accidentally struck a seven-year-old child with the tip of an umbrella. The boy cried; his mother frowned and rubbed his aching head. Standers-by explained to the parents that it had been an unintentional blow and that I am "a friend of the poor." I apologized. Both the mother and father smiled. Not always has the crowd stood with me, nor has understanding been so quickly shown. Although building trust is a missioner's task in Bangladesh, bestowing trust is the peoples' equally fine achievement.

Doing God's Will . . . Doing God's Work

October 31, 1998
Gaffargaon

Rasheeda, a four-year-old girl, had spurned food for a whole week and was starving. I pleaded with her mother to accompany me to the nutrition center where her daughter would recover. The woman refused because of fear of what men in the unknown city might do to her.

A young lady named Zulekha requested my help for burns she had received eleven years earlier. Now she wants her deformity corrected. It took me a few weeks and a bit of exertion to arrange with an accommodating surgeon for her treatment. On the appointed day, however, Zulekha did not appear.

I mentioned these incidents in letters to friends. By return mail they commented. "How depressing it must be to have your efforts rejected," and "It must be frustrating to be able to do so little for the people."

It is kind of friends to commiserate with me, but depressed and frustrated I am not. The truth is that I am steadily optimistic because I sense that I am doing with my life what God wants me to do. The Lord puts me in a position to mightily assist the bodily health, and save the lives, of many. Never mind that a mere fraction of the disabled and sick take advantage of my offer to aid them or that numerous others fail to follow through after all has been readied for them. I strive to be helpful. Some folks accept; others refuse. I have learned to understand that many of the Muslims I want to help are so suspicious of missioners that they are incapable of using me as I wish to be used, that is, for their own welfare. Foreigners are not automatically trustworthy in a country having a colonial history. Also, it is a widely held belief that "Christians only help Muslims in order to convert them to their religion."

It heartens me that lots of Muslims do, indeed, welcome my willingness to assist them as a brother. Some of them regain their health and begin to live fuller lives. On the other hand, some persons I have "helped" get worse; some die. Critics and other onlookers observe that I persist in trying to help. For them, even my unsuccessful attempts to save instill the lesson that Christians highly value Muslim lives.

A debate about the reason for "the vocation crisis" in the church: One opinion is that few persons are drawn to the priesthood because most priests do not adequately proclaim the joy that they feel. So, for the record: I'm happy. As a matter of fact, you may not know anyone happier than I am. This happiness has more to do with inner peacefulness than with frequent smiles. From time to time I ask myself: Why am I so happy? Is it because Maryknoll and the Bishop of Mymensingh enable me to restore and save physical lives as the major focus of my work? Or is it because Muslims and Hindus accept this witness of a life lived among and for them with ever-growing openness and approval? Is it because I have the freedom to go

on all-day bicycle rides to search for mostly young, inca-
pacitated persons? Or is it due, instead, to having a ready
audience with whom to discuss values and the purpose
of human life any time I wish to join Muslims in places
where they congregate? Or is it possibly because I so rel-
ish being a surprise to many people, including some local
Christians? All of those and many other aspects of life in
Bangladesh are indeed enjoyable and pep me up. Nevertheless, the prime reason for happiness in this missioner's
life is that I am doing God's will. I am aware that God uses
me for godly, neighborly purposes: to listen and love, to
serve and save, and to teach.

When on October 31, 1956 (I was a sophomore in college, then, and feeling miserable), I first responded to
the Attractive One, I envisioned a rather short period
of earthly labor to be followed by an eternity of intense
happiness. It only dawned on me a few years ago how
wonderfully happy I already am. Is one foot already in
Paradise? All I can say for sure is that this way of life is full
of purpose and, therefore, vastly rewarding. Gratitude is
probably the foremost charism God gives me. Enduring
thankfulness to the Attracting One keeps me in mission.

Bengalis habitually question me: "Why do you stay?
Is it because Bangladesh is the most beautiful country in
the world?" I reply: "Your country is indeed lovely. However, the reason I stay is not that but, rather, because of
the prolific opportunities to relieve hurt. For a Christian,
helping persons in distress is a profoundly religious act.
Serving the poor as Jesus did is the way Allah wills for me
to spend my life." They dearly love to hear it.

Occasionally, I return to visit the five towns where for-

merly I dwelt. Each time it strikes me that so many faces are new. How quickly a new generation replaces an old one in Bangladesh. It affects me that some young married women have died since my previous visit. I shall try to get to know the new partners of my old friends. Life goes on. In a milieu of need and struggle a missioner could die without being upset by the prospect. This feeling is beautiful and not at all morbid. The poor and I are essentially equals. I am part of a people, and there is no chasm between us. All of us belong to God.

A volley of greetings met me recently as I began visiting the neighborhood in Kishoreganj town where I lived ten years ago. Many held out their hands to be shaken. One man accompanied me on the trail. Just before we separated at a fork in the path he voiced an appraisal both plain and piercing: "When you come back here to see us it is a return to your family." Nice that he feels that way. So do I. I reckon mission in Bangladesh is about just that: demonstrating that Muslims, Hindus, and Christians are one family, already, and not merely potentially united in the indefinite future.

"The one who saves a person's life saves all of humankind." This gem of Jewish wisdom urges me to constantly make a start. Humankind is one. We are all related; we're family. Here is a chance to save the family. The love of Christ impels us.

Frailty Is No Bar to Bravery

October 31, 1999
Gaffargaon

Missioners frequently claim that they receive more from the people they have come to serve than they give to them. That claim, it seems to me, is not exaggeration.

After living four months in a new town, Gaffargaon, I was finally invited by a poor family to build a dwelling on the northern side of their tiny property. When Subhan and I had finished constructing a bamboo hut, his wife invited Jolil Munshi to read the Quran inside my new abode and to invoke an Islamic blessing upon it. For many of my neighbors, I am the first Christian they had ever met, and expected that I would also read from the Bible and offer a Christian blessing. Thus, the hut is doubly blessed by the Best Protector. In addition, I feel fortunate to have neighbors who, though illiterate and impoverished, are generally open-minded, restrain their anti-Christian prejudices, and accept me as a man.

On the railroad station platform I met a turbaned man, baggily clothed in wrinkled white cottons and wearing rings on every finger. His cloth shoulder bag had patches on patches. Mannan conversed enthusiastically about the myriad tombs of Muslim saints to which he goes on pilgrimage. This pilgrim's heart is with Allah and the saints. While the people of this town can hardly satisfy their curiosity about my purpose among them, I consider Mannan's lifestyle equally as fascinating. One day, I learned why Mannan had never invited me to his home. I saw my friend curled up and asleep on the grass. Mannan has no home and no special place to lay his head.

A blind, 25-year-old man, his wife, their infant daughter, and I made the chilly 6:30 a.m. rail journey into the city. Kashem, the unseeing one, received no encouragement from the doctors for the recovery of his sight. As we left the hospital together Kashem made a single request of me. "Please give me a sweater to relieve my shivering." Gladly I gave it. Not many persons in this world will settle for a garment to assuage their loss of vision.

Anxiously I awaited the arrival of Rubel and his parents so that we could catch the train to Dhaka. But when the train reached the station they were still nowhere in sight. Standing nearby, a complete stranger grasped that I was holding tickets for the soon-to-depart train and that I could still recover my expenses by selling them quickly to people crowded around the ticket window. He did not want to see me lose 60 takas ($1.20) in unused tickets. I am grateful to people who give unsolicited good advice and are genuinely concerned for me.

The deep tube well from which I and my neighbors must draw water is quite inconvenient. This source of water can be reached only by moving cautiously along sixty yards of narrow, uneven, slippery ridge which would try a goat's skill. Farida, mother of Shanu, has been bringing a potful of the precious fluid each day to my door. Allah bless her. When she arrived one day lugging the water-pot on her hip, she was wet and muddy. "I slipped!" she admitted with laughter. I deduce that Farida is my better. In similar circumstances I would not even grin.

Without notifying my friends, I appeared in Tangail for a twice-yearly visit. After borrowing Mukut's bicycle, I rode to Halim and Nilima's house to see about a place to stay overnight. But they were away, so I proceeded to the quarters of Mofiz. How impressive was his family's reception! After treating me exuberantly to the evening meal they had prepared for themselves, Mofiz's four daughters fed their brother, and only after that did they eat, sharing what the men had left. These folks are happier to offer hospitality than to fill their own stomachs. They amaze and humble me.

When I went to view the corpse of Farook, I said a few words to his grieving father. But when I came to Shereen, his 23-year-old widow, I was at a loss for words. Finally, I mumbled a dumb question, "How are you?" She replied, using the acceptable formula, "By the grace of Allah I am well." I wish I had not stumbled into asking that inept question, for the bereaved woman surely did not feel well. But she did know how to return a genteel answer even when the inquirer put a witless question.

Sharifa, a twelve-year-old girl who was scalped when her long, braided hair got caught in a rice-milling motor, came looking for me while I was away. She told the neighbors she had no place to stay the night before accompanying me to the hospital. Thus, they invited her to stay with them. Lovely initiative! I much admire that sort of sharing: a safe shelter with a mat and a pillow offered by the poor to the poor.

Renu, a slight, dark, pretty sixteen-year-old girl, had cirrhosis of the liver. She was pleased whenever I would visit and gently slap my baseball cap on her head. One day, I found her in pain, lying outdoors with an old umbrella shading her rapidly ageing face. "I've never had a *sharee* of my own," the dying lass declared. "Would you rather have additional medicine, or a *sharee*?" I asked. "A *sharee*!" she shot back. "A pink *sharee*," she added with a smile. After I had been to ten *sharee* shops I found an entirely pink one. Renu got up from her mat and let women drape her with her first *sharee*. I took some photos; she posed good-naturedly. Renu accepted that she would die within a fortnight. Frailty is no bar to bravery.

On several occasions I had instructed Ali to pick up

medicines that I had purchased for his daughter, Renu. Ali failed every time. Thus, when we chanced to meet on the street I scolded him straightaway. Finally, when he could get in a word edgewise, Ali told me with tears: "Renu died three days ago." As I was kicking myself for rashly complaining, Ali graciously insisted that I go to their hut on the morrow to eat a meal. Ali forgave and forgot my rashness.

The rickshaw-puller I hired to convey me to the rail station was in distress. His swollen, ulcerated right foot had been run over, he told me. The man needs hospitalization and, I suspect, a skin graft. Meanwhile, he pumps that cycle with all his strength and hopes that the foot will get better spontaneously. Surely the poor depend on God more than I do. Having no cash, they must rely wholly on the Merciful One.

Anoara, mother of three, told me something nice: "I dreamed last night about Bidya and Amiyo." Those two major seminarians had each spent several weeks living with me and befriending Muslims earlier this year. Anoara's dream affirms them; it indicates respect and affection. I must remember to tell the young Christian men that they are so highly esteemed. Every opportunity should be used to wean priests-to-be from their near total dependence on fellow Christians for moral support. Muslims are also our family, and future priests should feel that kinship.

Every day I experience encounters with goodness such as the above. The Author of all goodness works through Muslims and awakens in me awareness of their virtues. The church instructs me not only to acknowledge the

spiritual and moral goodness of Muslims but also to preserve and promote it. Sincere affirmation of the beauty in
Muslims' lives gives witness to the Truth, that is, to Jesus,
the One who came among us not to condemn but to save.

All His Pleasures Are Simple

October 31, 2000
Gaffargaon

Twenty-seven months ago when I moved to Gaffargaon
town I prayed that God would quickly insert me here
among the poor. In the beginning, I lived with two middle-class families. At Maeen Uddin's I had a room for one
month, and for the next three months I stayed at Farhat's.
Then, after four months of searching for a poor family
that would welcome me, I finally received an invitation to
build a small house in the compound of Subhaan and his
wife, Korful, and their extended family.

Before I could accept Subhaan's offer I had to caution
him. I am here to serve the seriously sick and disabled
poor, I explained. Allah's blessing is the only reward I
receive for this service. Allah's blessing—but no other
material benefits—I will share with you in return for
your hospitality. Subhaan agreed with my proposal even
though, at that early date in our acquaintance, he may

have imagined that I would bring to him more than mere spiritual gain. His family knows, of course, that one day I shall leave Gaffargaon and at that time the house I paid for will become theirs. By that time, however, the bamboo hut for which I spent $58 will probably require $50 worth of repairs. Bamboo rots. The poor have no lasting homes.

Promptly I learned to respect Subhaan's skill as a professional builder of houses. The way he wove strands of bamboo, using toes and fingers to hold and weave, fascinated me. His self-assured use of the short-handled scythe-like *dao* to smooth, chop, and notch the posts and braces was more than deft. It startled me to observe the dangerous tool in his fast, competent hands. He does all things well.

Subhaan (his name, in Arabic, means "glorifying") stutters when excited. The ordinary quarrels that arise in daily home life expose his nervous reaction. Thus, I was amazed one day when a young man urgently sought him because of a snake bite he had suffered. Subhaan swung into action using herbs and twine, but most of all, incantations. During twenty minutes, Subhaan, the snake-bite healer, prayed a blue streak over the frightened fellow, and not once did his voice falter. It was as if he had put on another personality; he spoke with authority.

Early in our relationship we had a clash about the outhouse. The extended family, that is, people from five houses, all share the same privy. When I arrived, I contributed money to hire a man who would empty the pit, and for the repair of its dilapidated walls. Nevertheless, soon afterward, Subhaan was after me to contribute again for the same purpose. We were at an impasse. Meanwhile, the hopper was overflowing. I insisted that I had done my share, and, finally, he relented. There had been no shouting between us, but we had taken one another's measure. Because he is Bengali, he had to test the limits of my openhandedness.

Subhaan works whenever he can get it, even at night time. Weaving bamboo by the light of a wick dipped into a wee can-full of kerosene has weakened his 46-year-old eyes. He asked me to help him. At the eye hospital in Mymensingh, 25 miles away, an eye exam cost 20 takas (40 cents U.S.), and the spectacles we bought cost 140 takas ($2.80). It made me happy to assist Subhaan in a way that will lengthen his work life. Two months later, he requested me to buy him another pair. The original pair had been stolen. I was less happy this time, but eventually relented.

In a village five miles away, a twenty-year-old man had fallen out of a tree and "broke his back," according to the local parlance. I took the youth and his father to the finest center in all of Bangladesh for spinal injuries. Three or four months of rehabilitation would be needed. Five days later, the father came to complain to me. The treatment was taking too long; he wanted to bring his son home now. I tried to dissuade him. He retaliated by reporting me to the police. Not finding me at home, the police hauled in Subhaan to interrogate him about his foreign guest. Perhaps, they suggested, this stranger who poses as a missionary is a kidnapper. Subhaan did not feed their suspicions.

Subhaan and I worked together again after the termites destroyed the original walls of my hut. I had not counted on the presence of these critters because I had not encountered them previously while building bamboo huts in four other towns. However, I had never lived in a place as muddy as Gaffargaon. So, we marched side by side to the bamboo market and bought several hard, heavy, twenty-foot-long lengths of the world's most useful grass. Subhaan, 5'3" tall and weighing one hundred pounds, led as we walked back home, half a kilometer away. The fat end of the bamboo rested squarely on his head. I followed, twelve feet behind, shouldering a lighter load. Even as he bore the awkward burden, his bearing, as usual, was dignified.

Whenever Subhaan is out of work and worried about how he will feed Shah Alom and Fulsum, their youngest son and daughter, he walks to the town's bazaar to look at the things he wishes he could buy. On rare occasions when he has an extra taka in the pocket of his blue shirt, he stops to savor a cup of tea and to observe foot traffic in the bazaar. There is not a better show in town even though there are three cinema halls. He loves to hold Milon, his granddaughter, and to ask her, "Where is your grandpa?" All his pleasures are simple.

Subhaan can neither read nor write, but already he has accomplished in life some of the essential deeds by which a Muslim Bengali is judged by his peers. Three years ago, he "gave away" their eldest daughter, Rokeya, by providing her with a dowry. The young man he found for her is a decent provider. Recently, he arranged for the circumcision of Shah Alom, age twelve. The ceremony is best performed when a boy is eight, but not all fathers can afford a festive meal at the best time. Bengali Muslims say that it is through the ceremony of circumcision that mere boys

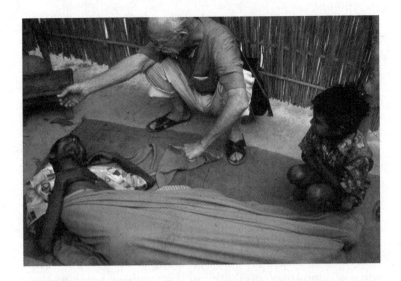

become Muslim boys, and it is the father's obligation to assure that it happens. By fulfilling that obligation Subhaan favored their son with the choicest gifts: Islamic faith and solidarity with Muslims everywhere.

Not long ago, a great African statesman died. His death sparked an outpouring of favorable comments from his missioner friends. That occurrence caused me to reflect that every single life is remarkable. Missioners are privileged to live among, serve, and be edified by the poor. We should have an aptitude for seeing and noting dignity and greatness in the lives of the deprived.

Subhaan and Korful, the poor, unschooled Muslim couple who accepted me into their compound nearly two years ago, gave me the opening that I needed in order to share, to a limited extent, in their lives. I apply to them the words from John's Gospel: "He who accepts anyone I send accepts me, and in accepting me accepts him who sent me." By receiving me into their lives, it seems clear from this passage, my closest neighbors, who remain proudly Muslims, accept Jesus and the One who sent him. Wouldn't you say so, too?

A Bamboo Hut Next to Theirs

October 31, 2001
Feni

Three months ago, I informed Bishop Francis that I would soon leave Mymensingh Diocese in order to witness elsewhere. "The door is always open for you," he graciously responded, assuring me that I could return at any time to the area in which I had already completed 25 years while living in six districts. A few days later—thanks to Habib, a man inspired by Allah to help me find shelter—I inserted myself into another district town 165 miles to the southeast. Feni town of Feni District is part of Chittagong Diocese, to which Bishop Patrick now welcomes me to serve the sick and live among the poor.

Immediately I began to inquire about and make contact with cleft-lip children, notifying their families about the free treatment available for them. I chose to start in the new district by aiding persons having this disfigurement because the results are plain to see and quick. Thus will

97

the people of Feni swiftly understand my intention to be useful to the poor, freely and as a brother.

During these first weeks I am living in a rented room provided by a middle-class family, for this is the normal way for me to begin in a totally unfamiliar town. For the time being, therefore, I dwell in a room having a cement floor and an indoor toilet, conveniences that I hope to be delivered from as soon as a poor family will invite me to build a bamboo hut next to theirs.

With me in the room are a bedroll and mosquito net, a bucket for drinking water, a kerosene stove with a cooking pot, a tin box that shields books and papers from rodents and cockroaches, one toad, and a bicycle. By bus I had hauled the bicycle to Feni. Nothing else that I might bring to this place could be more advantageous for the

poor. It is a most valuable tool for an apostolate on the highways and byways in search of the infirm and disabled. Whenever people in the countryside or the town ask for the address of my office I simply point to the two-wheeler: "This is my office."

A missioner expects every new place of abode to be different from its predecessors. Feni is as exceptional as any other town in which I have lived. Events and persons can still startle me. During more than a quarter of a century my motives for extending a hand to the poor who are Muslims were initially suspected by most of those whom I came to serve. I would, for example, be in a village inquiring about Abdul Mannan in order to assist his disabled child. Upon reaching the village I would inquire, "Where does Mannan live?" People's customary responses were: "Why do you want to know?" and "What is your connection to him?" Villagers protected one another from mistrusted outsiders. They wanted to be satisfied that I was not a collector who had come from a bank. Here in Feni, however, men generally dish out at once the directions I need. They might inquire, afterward, about my purpose with Mannan, but they do not make my explanation a condition for giving me accurate information. In Feni there appears to be a tendency to credit a foreigner with benign intentions. It's refreshing. This is the single most astounding difference between the towns I have lived in and the place where I now dwell.

When I returned to my room from the bazaar recently, I noticed a smiling, comely twelve-year-old lass directly behind me. She had, it seems, followed me from the alley and all the way to my door. "Is there something?" I queried. "I just want to meet you. My name is Navila," she explained. Saying that, she held out her hand for me to shake. Which I did, but my eyebrows were arched. Female-initiated handshakes probably mean that television programs are not merely watched; they are studied and imitated.

Shaon, a bright, healthy student of class four, offered me a lighted mosquito coil during my first afternoon in the rented room. "Thank you," said I. "You are welcome," he responded, thereby bowling me over. I do not recall the last time I heard those three little words in Bangladesh. In the places I have lived, "thanks" and "you're welcome" are rarely heard. Rather, a recipient's debt of gratitude simply perdures, and is unremarked. Hence, when I described Shaon's courtesy to a fellow missioner, he dubbed Feni "cosmopolitan."

In the vegetable bazaar I selected some potatoes for the attendant to weigh. Indignantly he tossed the spuds back into his basket and gestured for me to take a hike. Mystified by his huffiness I calmly insisted to know "What did I do wrong?" He instructed me irately: "In this town the storekeeper chooses the vegetables; the customer takes what he gets." That staggered me. Unexcitedly I related to him the custom of the Mymensingh area, where for twenty-five years I observed customers picking out their own potatoes. Unexpectedly he mellowed, and picking up the two large spuds I had originally chosen, weighed them and dropped them into my shopping bag. He seemed pleased that I had taken the time to inform him, and to be informed by him. Patience paid off. Occasionally I restrain my annoyance and thereby surprise myself.

Shajahan, a twenty-year-old student of Arabic and Islamics, is an intelligent fellow preparing for a lifetime of religious leadership in the Islamic community. The other day he came looking for me in my room while I was away. He left a note, which I received hours later, but which I was unable to decipher. A neighbor made out the atrociously misspelled words for me. "How is it possible," I marveled out loud, "that a person so highly educated is so feeble in the Bengali language?" My neighbor gave a sidelong glance and explained with scorn: "Our religious professionals customarily do not study our language and literature." How then, I ask myself, can they lead Bengalis, a people enormously proud of their mother tongue?

During my first week in Feni I was enlightened by several keen observers of the local scene. Kashem related that "Here there are no religious fanatics." He went on, however, to negate that advantage with a statistic: "In the past five years politically motivated violence has claimed the lives of 54 members of one party and 34 members of their rival party." In other words, here fanaticism is political. Moreover, since having that conversation the number of slain has grown by fifteen. Feni, I observe, is referred to in the national press as "the country's most troubled district."

Azad coolly summarized his feelings about the place: "Feni is an agitated place. So, Brother Bob, I request you to move to my district (250 miles northwest of here) where you will have unlimited scope for serving the poor." It is thoughtful of the man to invite me. He appreciates my purpose. But first let me try to contribute something to this intriguing place.

How Good It Is for Us to Be Here

October 31, 2002
Feni

All my neighbors are Muslims. The compound where I live with forty rickshaw drivers and two families consists of two long tin sheds, a hand-operated water pump, and one toilet.

News of the catastrophe on September 11, 2001, reached us within hours. For several weeks most Bangladeshis could think only sympathetically of the victims. However, when the victimized nation began to retaliate, the perception of my acquaintances was that now the Afghan poor, persons who had already suffered too much, had become the newest targets of vengeance. My neighbors saw, and see, no justification for killing anyone besides the evildoers.

On a Friday after bombs began to fall on Afghanistan I went to the pond to bathe. Nearby, an officer of the mosque, with microphone in hand, was calling the faithful to community prayer. He was also giving them the lowdown on Americans, exhorting Muslims to remember: "America is a Christian country. They have refused to accept Islam and, therefore, they kill Muslims." I asked myself: "Should I go over there, cite facts and use logic to explain another side of the story?" Prudence answered me: "No crowd coming out of the mosque after prayer is hoping to hear your views. Finish your bath and go home."

Bangladeshis like to use amplifiers, stationary or mounted on rickshaws, to popularize their causes. On the main street of the town it puzzles no one to behold an excited critic excoriate "the killers of innocent Muslims" while not far away a hawker offers printed forms for sale which, when filled out and posted to Washington, DC, may make the applicants eligible "to live in the United States of America."

On a visit to Barisal town I met with Kamrul, a successful teacher and tutorial school owner whom I had befriended 25 years ago. Kamrul has always been most cordial toward me. Yet, as we shared rice and curry in his home, he could not repress the urge to rebuke what he perceives as American arrogance: "Why is it that the U.S. government will not show us the alleged proof of bin Laden's guilt?"

Educated Muslims condemn the September 11 attacks. Intellectually, they deplore the killing of blameless persons. But on the gut level, it seems to me, many of them admire the man and organization that finally captured American attention. Their Islamic community throughout the world harbors grievances. America's resolute siding with Israel against Palestine and sanctions against Iraq, which they view as depriving food and medicine to kids, are two of them. Thus, they do not bemoan actions that humiliate America. Humiliating the superpower is what they like about September 11, and not the stark bloodiness of that day—as if one could ignore the gore while relishing the dashed invulnerability of the world's mightiest nation.

Two doctor friends who have been helpful to me and the sick poor whom I serve gave me counsel. Tarek was pessimistic about both the world and local situation since September 11 and wanted me to be extra careful. Hanif had knowledge of Bangladeshi students of religion who had received training in Afghanistan, and he advised me frankly: "Take a three months' leave in the United States until things cool off here." They know how easy it would be for someone to erase a lone foreigner and how little would be done about it afterward.

Days before receiving their advice, as I was bicycling through villages west of Feni town, I was taunted and sneered at. At a village doctor's office I was received more coolly than on a previous affable visit. "Americans are killing ordinary people, people without fault," he sternly reminded me. In another village, one in which I had never been before, a youth led me through a crowd that had gathered to inspect me. "Where is he from?" someone asked knowingly. My guide lied without hesitation to protect me: "He is Japanese."

Occasionally I meet someone who is so intrigued by my purpose to live as Jesus did that he accompanies me in order to explain to his fellow Muslims, thereby helping them to understand and trust me. It happened again a few months ago in Elahiganjo village. A welder named Bahar joined me on his bicycle to search for persons in need of surgical attention. In every home or bazaar Bahar broke the ice for me. After explaining to them that I live with the poor and stay in Bangladesh in order to be useful to persons in need, he answered peoples' queries about me, sometimes accurately. The essential points, however, he never missed: service and simplicity.

Someone wrote from America to tell me he thinks I am "soft on Islam." What he means by that I think I grasp. What is it, I ask myself, that inspires benevolent thoughts in a Christian missioner toward the Muslims of Bangladesh? The manifest goodness of so many persons fuels my respect for them. For the most part, they are tolerant, hospitable, and attuned to the Compassionate One. Even if I had never read a book about Islam I would have noticed these characteristics in Bengali Muslims. In fact, in my view, reading others' descriptions of Islam is not the preferred way to learn about Muslims. Why not simply meet Muslims? The reason I respect Islam and admire many

Muslims is because I have gotten to know them during more than a quarter of a century, and they are good.

Another letter from America reached me early this year seeking understanding of Muslims. "In your experience are Muslims eager to cooperate with other religious groups, or do you get the feeling they want to eliminate all but Islamic believers?" I replied: "Neither of the above. The Muslims I know are not eager to engage in interreligious dialogue or to cooperate with non-Muslim believers. Muslims feel their religion totally adequate. They also suspect that Christians may try to use togetherness with Muslims as the first step in a process of converting Muslims. So, they think: 'Why expose ourselves? We don't need phony togetherness.' On the other hand, I do not get the impression that many Muslims want to eliminate Christians. The sort of person who belittles and blasts Christians, using microphone and amplifier to stir hatred in the hearts of fellow Muslims, might wish for the elimination of Christians. But their number is small. (And does anyone doubt there are Christians who wish Islam were eliminated?) The Prophet of Islam instructed Muslims to look after the safety of believers in other faiths wherever Muslims are in the majority. In the spirit of that teaching, Bangladeshi Muslims permit Christian missioners to live in their midst and witness to Jesus in deeds and words. I consider that it has never been truer than now to say. 'How good it is for us to be here.'"

Our Exertions Give Witness to Allah's Mercy

October 31, 2003

Feni

Bicycling in an alley of Feni town I encountered a large, black-bearded man, piously dressed and wearing a severe expression on his face. After staring at me a while his face suddenly softened. He smiled broadly, gestured expansively, and declared "Thank you." I did not know the man or why he felt friendly toward me. Maybe he had heard that I have helped numerous Muslim children who are disabled. His frank appreciation for someone outside his own religious, ethnic, and cultural communities is basic to building peace. I think of him as a provocateur of harmony between Muslims and Christians.

Several seminarians have come to dwell in Feni for a fortnight each, assigned by their superiors to live with me among Muslims, up close. One of the young men, Dominic, is a competent cyclist but unaccustomed to riding long distances. For his sake I almost regretted one day that we rode twenty miles to perform tasks that could have been done in ten. I consoled him with the fact that even when we merely ride, and are apparently only exercising, we actually never waste time while going around. "So, then," he reasoned, "if we would ride motorbikes we could go farther and see even more people." True, I argued, but bicycles are a simpler technology, more suited to showing our oneness with the poor. To the Muslims our exertions give witness

107

to Allah's mercy, a concept about which they have heard much from their Islamic faith.

Another seminarian, Pradip, was with me when several men stopped us in the bazaar. They had lots of questions for us about lifestyle, for example, celibacy, living among the poor, and cooking for ourselves. The men could hardly believe that they heard us say about service to the poor being sufficient cause for our happiness in this life. What sort of spirituality is this, they seemed to be thinking, that makes what you do for others the measure of your happiness?

A fire was burning in the earthen stove where rice was being cooked for the fifty rickshaw drivers with whom I share this compound. Thus, I carried waste papers from my room to the cooking shed to feed to the flames. Normally this act of neighborliness is welcomed. Not, however, this time. Noor Islam, a rickshaw driver, spied among the papers I was tossing out a small empty carton having familiar writing on it. "Arabic," he announced. "The Quran." (In fact, the script was Urdu, which looks similar.) I explained: "The writing you see is merely about the spices that once filled this carton." Nevertheless, I quietly withdrew the carton. My closest Muslim neighbors are mostly illiterate. They have been taught that Arabic is a holy script, not fit to be consigned to fire, especially by a Christian.

During Ramadan, the month of fasting and special attention to prayer, numerous men of Noor Islam's neighborhood are glad for my presence because they like to have someone on whom to exercise their piety. They enjoy instructing me not to wash my clothes or bathe my body at the pond beside the mosque because the noise disrupts their prayer. Several times I arrived at the pond half an hour before prayers—plenty of time to wash clothing and take a bath before their prayers. What happened? Persons old and young warned me not to transgress the demands of Islamic devotion. Zeal for prayer consumes them.

One evening, as I walked slowly along the unlighted road in front of our compound, a rickshaw pulled alongside. The driver, from another compound and unknown to me, sternly informed me of the displeasure he feels whenever he sees me: "Your countrymen are killing Muslims!" Bangladeshi Muslims, as probably Muslims of many nations, have a consciousness that they belong to a worldwide community. When one part of the community is grievously hurt, all suffer—like a body. I was not disappointed when the complainer disappeared into the darkness after getting off his chest that which readily inflames his emotions.

At noonday soon after the invasion of Iraq, I was cursed and mocked. I was returning to my own neighborhood after biking afar all morning. Someone shouted *"Haram-jada!,"* a term of abuse, like "scoundrel!" or worse. Shortly afterward, while I bathed in the pond another sneered loudly, "Bob Bush!" At neither of the detractors did I look. They knew I had heard them and that I was not ignoring them but, rather, was absorbing their disgust. Whenever I can I try to remain silent under abuse. That way the initiative remains with the abusers; any escalation of incivility will have to be theirs. Moreover, I trust in their decency not to overdo the abuse.

In a letter from America a friend implored me to come

home: "If you are harmed now it is surely political, not about faith." The statement illustrates that my friend does not share the Bengali Muslims' mentality. For, to these Muslims politics and faith are intertwined. Naturally, they imagine that Americans feel the same way. Bengali Muslims say and think, "Americans are Christians." Thus, what is done to Americans is perceived as done to Christians.

Besides war, there are other issues that try the Bengalis' tolerance. The presence of poisonous arsenic in the drinking water all over Bangladesh is a recently proven reality. Myriad hand pumps, called shallow tube wells because they deliver water from depths of forty to sixty feet, had saved the nation from cholera and diarrhea over the years. But now we have learned those tube wells are dangerous for the arsenic-laced water they give. The NGO for which Nizam and Feroz work has already installed a few hundred deep tube wells to compensate for the tens of thousands of arsenic-contaminated shallow tube wells. One of their new, 773-foot-deep wells is 200 yards away. "Would you not prefer to drink safe water?" they graciously offered. Indeed, and thank you. Nevertheless, no one should be surprised if millions of Bangladeshis contract arsenic poisoning.

Imam Hossain, a disabled shoe repairman, stood up hastily when he saw me drawing near. "Brother! I have two patients for you. One child has a cleft lip. The other child has a bloated leg. Can you help them?" We arranged for the two children from distant villages to meet me on a Thursday. "Brother," Imam continued, "let me give you tea. You helped my son, now I want to treat you." I assured Imam that his searching for others to help was all the reward I want. "Now, Imam, you and I are partners striving together for others." How marvelous it is when persons of vastly different backgrounds unite to relieve others of their burdens!

Direction That Matters, Not the Distance

October 31, 2004
Gaibandha

"You are going to the poorest district in all Bangladesh," an attendant at the Dhaka bus terminal told me. Although I suspected he was exaggerating, it was reassuring to hear his appraisal of Gaibandha, the district town situated in northwest Bangladesh to which I moved that day.

Four years previously, Bishop Moses had invited me to join this diocese. Several months later, while I was still missioning in the nation's southeastern diocese, a discerning friend named Azad attracted me to the northwest, saying, "You will have greater scope there for service to the poor." How fortunate for me that when I arrived on Azad's doorstep, three years after he had enticed me to relocate, he spontaneously offered me shelter! Until the current monsoon season ends and flood waters recede I shall be unable to build an abode of my own. Meanwhile, Azad unselfishly shares his house with me.

Immediately upon arriving in Gaibandha I began going around, by bicycle, through countless villages, explaining to many who asked about my identity and purpose: "I am a Christian missionary; the well-being of your disabled ones is my purpose for coming to you." Initially my outreach is toward persons having cleft lips. Thus, every Friday night, accompanied by two cleft-lipped children and their parents, we travel to Dhaka, where Doctor Khundkar, a splendid plastic surgeon, competently and freely repairs them. In Gaibandha, a place having neither Christians nor other missionaries, the effort to assist persons having cleft lips is an excellent and quick means to help the community understand that the missioner has come in order to make happier the lives of persons who are neglected.

In the villages I meet and speak with numerous men and boys, frequently as they sit in or stand around dingy bamboo tea stalls. Paid professional performers sometimes deliver their lines before smaller crowds. It is so easy to find a listening audience in Bangladesh. All that are needed are a willingness to submit oneself to scrutiny and a grasp of the Bengali language. With those assets a person will normally be received, respected, and responded to. The inquisitive nature of the Bengali people fosters dialogue; dialogue, in turn, promotes harmony.

After two months in Gaibandha I had not yet been able to discover a dry plot of land on which to construct a wee house. Thus, I was still not cooking my own meals; I took breakfast and supper in restaurants. At the conclusion of supper one day a lone businessman sitting across the aisle

taunted me several times, "Al Qaeda!" He did not say he thought that entity to be good, or bad. He merely wished to see my reaction. All I could muster was a raised eyebrow. Seeing my taciturnity, another well-dressed fellow interrupted my meal, smiling grandly in my face and warning, "The Taliban is looking for you." Well, until the day I can erect a hut and start to do my own cooking there, lots of folks know I sup daily around 4:00 p.m. at the Food Village restaurant, and that even Talibanis (if such exist in Gaibandha) are also welcome there.

In the bazaar of village Horina it pleased me to experience the broad-mindedness of Ruhul Amin, owner of a small store. I had hardly finished explaining myself to a cluster of men beside his store. Never having seen a Christian missionary before, most of the men were hindered from fathoming what I told them. Perhaps my appearance threw them off; surely my proclamation did, that is: "The purpose of life is to love, and authentic Islam and Christianity must make us generous toward one another." Ruhul interpreted "missionary" for the group in terms of dedication to Allah and zeal for people's welfare. He truly understands the missioner's respect for Islam and for Muslims. He is, therefore, confident that no effort will be made to convert the poor, that is, the easily coerced ones, to another religion.

Close to village Datia I was bicycling along a murky, flooded pathway. As I advanced, the front wheel struck an obstacle that pitched me off balance. By jumping off quickly I landed on my feet, but the splash was enormous, covering me with muddy water. The surprising part for me was in experiencing the people's reaction. Normally in Bangladesh such mishaps elicit a torrent of jollity from spectators. But the response of the villagers was muted, not merry. Is Gaibandha a more genteel place than I have grown accustomed to? Or is it my age that moves people to make less fun of me than they otherwise might? I have friends who will blame me for not recognizing the obvious: as I get older, people have added regard.

On the way to village Simul Tari I recognized the road as one I had traveled one month earlier. I wished only to learn from the pedestrians I met how far I had yet to travel in order to reach my destination. Several replied, offering me directions. I protested to assure them I already knew this path and its direction, but did not know the distance to my goal. That explanation puzzled them. For Bangladeshi villagers it is the direction that matters, not the distance. Thus, if you are on the right path do not even bother to inquire how far you have yet to go. Surely you will reach that place. Just keep plodding ahead. Not a bad philosophy.

Early one morning, in Rifaitpur village, Shah Alam, the father of two children I had assisted, was walking beside me. His voice quivered as he exclaimed: "I shall never forget you for what you have done for my children. Their treatment was the greatest difficulty I was facing, and then an American came to be my brother." For all the criticism of America that Bangladeshi Muslims feel justified in declaring, there is also—especially among the less advantaged ones—a readiness to credit Americans.

By chance we met on a street in the town. There were Zulfiqur, Sufi, Monir and Ekram—businessmen, ages 35 to 45—who all knew of my quest for a bit of land, 8 feet by 10 feet, on which I could build a dwelling. We kidded a while—mostly about celibacy and my desire to live beside the poor—and then began to walk together, eastward toward Siddiq's compound, to investigate a place. That plot, however, was still under water. They pointed out that I could raise the level by using landfill. Nevertheless, I refused the place because there were no poor families on either side who would be my closest neighbors. Anyway, it makes me glad to experience the efforts of these men, Muslims who are trying to help a Christian missionary find a place to dwell among them.

Dialogue Promotes Harmony

October 31, 2005
Gaibandha

During the first five months of my stay in the new town, Gaibandha, ten persons offered to let me build a house on their land. One of them, Sohel, welcomed me with the understanding that I need not pay land rent. His family knows their only reward will be to share in the blessings Allah bestows on me for helping the disabled. In some of the other locations proposed to me by hospitable people I may have enjoyed more privacy or nicer scenery. However, at Sohel's I enjoy proximity to the town's bazaars and many nearby companions in a crowded neighborhood. Thus have I settled just across the tracks from the Gaibandha railway station.

The first stage of house building in this frequently flooded district is to lay an earthen foundation. Thus did Haidar cut and carry earth from 100 yards away. Within two days he raised by 18 inches the foundation of my 8-foot-by-10-foot plot, sufficiently high to keep my feet dry during a normal monsoon.

An expert bamboo craftsman named Noya Miah (that is, "Mr. New") then began to build. Fifteen days later I took possession of my dirt-floored, bamboo-walled home. People call it, not a house, but, rather, a hut, because the roof is of straw and not of galvanized iron—the favored building material. Total expenses for the hut and its foundation were $55.

The dwelling was prepared barely in time for me to receive the first of two theology students from the major seminary. Every day during Peter's seventeen-day sojourn we bicycled to villages, often stopping to answer questions. "Why do you inconvenience yourselves for others?" They wanted to know. "Jesus lived this way," we replied.

Later, David, another seminarian, was my partner when we found an old man lying in rags on the cold cement verandah of the railway station. Muhammad, as we dubbed him, tried to tell us who he was but was too weak to utter. We brought a burlap sack to place under his head as a pillow. When I pledged to return the next morning he stroked my forearm and guided my hand to his heart. On the third day of our attention to Muhammad a spectator informed us about a woman who had lugged a bucket of water to the verandah, removed most of the man's clothes, and bathed him. Then, she fed him.

Our informant declared, "She is not a good person!" We proposed otherwise: "If she bathes the soiled, feeds the hungry, and comforts the lonely, she surely is a very good person."

Water having a high iron content is a frequent source of stomach troubles in Bangladesh. Thus, the first home improvement I made was to build a water filter. Neighbor Alamgir helped me. Two months later, Alamgir, age 38, died of a stroke, leaving his widow with three children, ages seven, three, and six weeks. Many folks have come to console the family. Before they leave, they usually peek inside my hut. I point out the water filter Alamgir and I made together. They regard it with reverence.

Dulu, also of this neighborhood, had agreed to go with me to a hospital in Dhaka, six hours away, for her son's treatment. As the time approached for our journey it became clear that some people were nervous about it. Several women grilled me near the room Dulu shares with her parents and two small sons. Then, some men came to talk things over, along with Dulu and her mother, seeking assurances. "You must simply trust me," I counseled. Certainly they had never before entrusted a relative of theirs, that is, this young mother, to the guardianship of a stranger. It was hard for them. Yet, that is what I offer people: an opportunity to trust a stranger.

Several miles northwest of my home a tornado struck, uprooting trees, collapsing solid brick walls, and strewing mangled sheets of galvanized iron. The death toll was fifty. Many went from the town by bicycle, motorcycle, and train to view the devastation. In village Kishamot, a tiny table placed under the open sky became a makeshift tea stall. "Good for you!" I thought of the determined owner, for refusing to let the destruction of his former twelve-seat tea stall stymie his livelihood. I had been wondering what I might do for the tornado victims besides admire their resolve and industry. Several packets of biscuits stacked on the table suggested a way. Purchasing all the packets, I handed one to each of the five men and boys standing nearby. Upon seeing that kindness the tea stall owner blurted out: "Everyone has come here to look at us, but this man is doing some good!" I thank God for biscuits, which saved me from being completely useless to the afflicted.

One day, in village Kamar Para, I joined several men sitting in yet another tea stall. They questioned me and listened closely to the responses. "Which is the best of all countries? Do you have a degree? Why do you not marry?" We were having a lively exchange. After a while, they seemed almost persuaded that it is possible for a man inspired by Allah to renounce the blessings of marriage and to live celibately and happily for the One. But then, curry being prepared in the kitchen next door made me choke and cough. I had to vacate the premises and discontinue evangelizing because my eyes were watering and my lungs gasping for fresh air. When people talk about obstacles to spreading the Good News they seldom mention curry.

Another neighbor, Zilur, has epilepsy, which attacks in unpredictable places. Last month he suffered a fit while locked inside our common outhouse. Sohel had to rip off the door to rescue his cousin. More recently, as he was walking to the bazaar, Zilur collapsed and tumbled head-first into a flooded paddy field. A pair of alert teenagers saved him. One good feature about life in the world's most densely populated country is that one is never far from helpers.

Your Smiling in Your Brother's Face Is Charity

October 31, 2006
Gaibandha

"How long have you lived in Gaibandha?" someone asked me last July 9. Just then, it flashed into my mind: exactly two years earlier I had arrived in the unknown town. Customarily, in every one of the eight towns where I have settled, during my first year among them, many Muslims are suspicious of me, for they wrongly imagine the Christian missionary intends to convert them. Then, by the second year, their trust in me has grown. Finally, during the third year, many regard me affectionately. And so it happened in this town, also.

When I walk to the bazaar I often take a shortcut through the railway station. As I made my way along the station's platform recently, the morning train also pulled in. All disembarking passengers advanced toward the single exit, converging at the gate as does water when poured into a funnel. Jostled by the crowd, I also was carried along to the gate, where a lone, harried ticket gatherer was checking the validity of passengers' tickets. Busy though he was, he stopped the traffic, blocking the exit with his body and outstretched arms. Then, he smiled and greeted me cordially, "Peace be upon you." When I returned his peace wish, traffic resumed. Friendly folks here make time for civility.

While sitting in the open doorway of my hut I was sorting photographs. Fourteen-year-old Sheema saw me handling photos and rushed to my side. Just then, pious Hasan exited his house and, as he passed by, saw one of the cutest girls in the neighborhood looking over my shoulder at snapshots. "What are you doing here?" he demanded to know. Giggling, the girl did not reply. Hasan kept staring, displeased that a Muslim girl would be so curious about photographs. Sheema, however, did not retreat. Soon, Hasan tired of standing up for righteousness and moved along. The enforcers of propriety are not so strict on my associates.

As I sat writing notes for persons who had come to see me, the mosquitoes were biting my ankles. Ismael, grandfather of a disabled child, sat facing me in a squatting position. He was looking after three sets of ankles—the child's, his own, and mine. Now and then as I wrote I felt him gently slap my tormentors with his bare hand. In this culture—where touching others' feet is an act of humility—Ismael showed his warmth by driving away my pursuers.

Twice a year the whole nation is caught up in harvesting. Women and men, girls and boys—all have tasks. Everywhere, farmers stand threshing. The roads become covered with rice straw strewn there to dry beneath the sun. Bicycle riders have to spend extra energy to plow through the soft, deep straw. A woman threshing beside the road was tossing sheaves aside carelessly. One bundle, thrown with abandon, nearly hit me as I biked along. When our eyes met, she smiled brightly. It reminded me of her Prophet's saying: "Your smiling in your brother's face is charity."

While I was explaining to a crowd of villagers the possibility that a child standing in our midst could be cured by accompanying me to a hospital, an enthusiastic thirty-year-old man interrupted to address me. "I know you. You have come to serve the poor. You live like the poor in order to suffer with us. Thank you!" As he spoke a big smile lit his face, as if to say: "Don't deny what I say; I know all about you." When I rode away he spoke again, as if representing the village, "We thank you."

Saleh and I had not met for six months. He welcomed me into his home, exclaiming, "I am so happy to see you again!" Saleh, formerly a United Nations peacekeeper in Africa, imagined that we might not meet again in this life, so he spoke "from the core of my heart." The misunderstanding, which he perceives in the Western media, disturbs him, especially the caricature *Islamic terrorist*. He reasons, thus: "The people here, we all, love you and respect you for who you are. When I think of you, it is not as Saleh the Muslim and Bob the Christian, but simply as a friend. Is not Bangladesh the most loving place you have ever experienced? And we are mostly Muslims." When I stood to leave he shook my hand firmly and repeated with feeling, "I am so glad you came!"

I know better than to soap my back while standing in deep pond water because the bar might slip from my hand and fall irretrievably into murky water. Which is precisely what happened one day. My brief search was futile. But Chintu, a boy known as "retarded," observed me searching and came quickly to assist me. Within two minutes, Chintu emerged with my lost soap in hand. I invited him to come to my hut soon so I could take his snapshot. Solicitous children deserve recognition.

A few months ago I attended a celebration which Bishop Bejoy, the newest and youngest of our six diocesan bishops, also attended. While we sat together at table he merrily and publicly invited me to make my next move to his diocese. He even suggested a place for me—a district where no Christians live. How nice to be recruited to be a witness of God's love for the world.

Not long ago, I traveled to the district town of Rangpur to learn more about it. There, in the center of the town, I made an intriguing new acquaintance—a tall, dark, candid man who introduced himself as Monirul Kabir Jesus. I knew he was a Muslim because Christians in Bangladesh do not take the name Jesus. This Jesus showed me a handbill he had printed for distribution, about world peace, and signed "Jesus." When I introduced myself as a Christian missionary he straightaway urged me not to call myself merely "Bob Brother," but rather, Bob Jesu. It would not surprise me that people regard him as eccentric. Nevertheless, it is clear that he—and other Muslims, too—want me to live as did Jesus.

Muslims and Hindus Entertain Me on Their Holidays

October 31, 2007
Narail

"Anywhere you choose to settle, just let me know," Bishop Bejoy assured me when welcoming me to Khulna Diocese. Thus did I investigate six of the thirteen districts within the diocese. In every place I sought to learn whether or not Christians of any denomination reside there. In one of the six districts dozens of splinter groups within the same denomination exist. I wish to avoid living in such a place because Muslims will surely ask me to answer why so many divisions, and I cannot answer. At the beginning of the search, Narail was the district I was least inclined to choose because a priest of the diocese had previously told me of his intention to work for conversions there. Despite that prospect, and because Narail impressed me as the poorest of the six, I decided to try, with God's help, to insert myself there.

Happily, I soon found a room to rent. Momin agreed to let me stay in half of an old tin shed. Twice more I met with him to reconfirm our deal, but at our third meeting he suddenly reneged. I walked away dejected but decided not to be deterred. The first man who crossed my path I asked if he knew a place to rent. He didn't, but explained my problem to a passing cyclist. A minute later, the cyclist handed me over to an ice vendor, who interrupted his business dealings to connect me with a devout fellow just emerging from prayer at the mosque. That one walked me to the compound of Mohammad Khaybar. Khaybar was out, but I was assured a room by another renter. Several days later, I returned with bicycle and bedding to take possession of an 8 foot x 9 foot room having an earthen floor and no electricity. The rent is 200 takas per month,

that is, almost 10 cents U.S. per day. After the rains end I hope to build my own dwelling.

Without delay I started out on bicycle to get acquainted. Early journeys took me through villages named "Mystic," "Under the Mango Tree," "Cracked Head," and "Rotten." In every village, people wanted to know why I was there. As it creates suspicion in people's minds if a newcomer goes around merely looking, I needed a specific excuse for being there. "Are there persons here having cleft lips?" I inquired. Often, I stopped at schools to ask the teachers for help in identifying children in need of surgery or physiotherapy. At Mizpara High School the teachers were delighted to receive the elderly, slightly muddy foreigner. A female teacher, after learning my age, confessed eagerly, "Seeing you gives me energy!" Professionals like her regard bicycling afar not simply as transportation or exercise but as sacrifice.

During the flood season a large part of the district's population was harvesting and stripping jute plants. My first realization of how significant is the Hindu population of Narail came from observing a multitude of Hindu women and girls busy at this fieldwork. Muslim women do not, as a rule, work in the open, as were these women. Although on the national level only 9 percent of Bangladeshis are Hindus, I believe a retired education officer who calculates Narail has 40 percent. If that is so, this is the district having the highest percentage of Hindus in Bangladesh.

One day, as I stood in a store, a man introduced himself to me as "Hubert, a Christian." He told me about periodic visits made to Narail by missionaries from Khulna.

Probably they pay attention to this place because many people are poor (that is my reason, too), but also because it has so many Hindus—persons they perceive as potential converts to Christianity. The perception among some missionaries that poor persons of Hindu background are easier to convert than are Muslims is accurate. All the more reason for me to live among Muslims and Hindus simply as one devoted to the poor, but also as a missionary who has not the faintest intention to convert them.

Shoumen, my Hindu neighbor, invited me for a meal on the occasion of an Islamic festival. "But you are a Hindu," I reminded him. "What about my children?" he parried. "They see their Muslim neighbors eating in celebration, and they feel they should be eating, too. So, we celebrate Muslim festivals as well as the Hindu ones." Two days after accepting the hospitable Hindu's invitation thoughtful Muslim neighbors invited me for the same meal. I had to beg off and they understood. It makes sense to the Muslims that Hindus would entertain me on an Islamic holiday.

The room I live in is usually dark, so I sit outdoors to read. Normally, my silent presence draws curious children; sometimes it attracts numerous adults, mostly female, who gather to gab or to tease me. The first time it happened I rather enjoyed it, for Muslim women are expected to be reserved. We were discussing food preparation or some such pleasant topic when Begom asked: "What would you like for us to do with your body if you suddenly die here?" Although I recovered my composure quickly and reminded them neither I nor they would ever cease to live unto Allah, they had also reminded me that in Bangladesh teasing is not for the fainthearted.

Shameem, Begom's son, is eight years old and curious. One day, he declared to me, "Hello!" Then he asked me, "Uncle, what does 'hello' mean?" I explained what a greeting is, but it only confused him. Shameem had thought "Hello" means "Listen to me!" for that is the way he hears adults use the word, that is, to get others' attention. In this place the proper response to a sharp "Hello" is: "What would you like to say to me?"

Every six months I try to revisit the eight towns where I have dwelt since arriving in Bangladesh in 1975. Starting that journey at the Dhaka rail terminal recently, the train headed north. Within moments I sat staring out the open window at the drama of life on display. Families live quite near to the rail lines; in small, low-roofed bamboo huts squashed one against another, dwellings that offer a modicum of defense against monsoon rains and even less defense against heat. The sun at 7:30, beating on their bamboo and polythene roofs, had already driven most inhabitants outdoors. Arriving and departing trains frequently disrupt their lives and pose a constant danger for the children running freely within a few feet of the passing giants. During those first fifteen minutes of travel uncomplaining people mesmerized me. Although it made me sad to see them living in such conditions, my overriding emotion was not sadness. Though they live in suffocating closeness to others, they do so with dignity, and I am immensely proud of them.

Bangladeshis Respect Spiritual Motives

October 31, 2008
Narail

A group of educated, middle-class men beckoned me to come sit with them. They wanted to know, "Does being a Christian missionary mean you are here in Narail to convert people?" I responded: "It does not. I am here to live as a Christian and to be useful to the poor. There is no bad religion in Bangladesh." The men heartily agreed. One of them, Jamal, then and there offered me free use of a plot of land on which to build a house.

Alom and I worked six hours moving 150 cubic feet of earth (the foundation for my hut) to the plot given me. Alom is about 65; he is wiry, unschooled, has poor eyesight, and is expert and tireless when constructing a house made of bamboo (the frame) and jute sticks (the siding). His measurements made me anxious, for he used only a piece of string, or the length of his forearm, to measure pieces that had to be cut exactly. "You'll soon see what I mean," he repeatedly assured me. And so it happened; all the pieces fit. Moreover, the roof is of sticks covered by polythene, and it keeps me dry.

Gopal came from his village to see me in my house. The final one hundred meters was by way of a muddy path, causing him to arrive smudged. Before departing, he asked me, "Why do you live in such a place?" I explained that Jesus lived simply, with the poor, and the disciple is not greater than the master. That made sense to him because the reason is spiritual, not merely practical. Bangladeshis, both Muslims and Hindus, respect spiritual motives.

During a bus ride to Jessore, a bearded, piously dressed Muslim sat beside me. Dhaheedul asked whether I had read the Quran. I had indeed. "Did you like what you read?" he inquired expectantly. "The Quran and Islamic preaching in general do not attract me," I told him frankly. "What is inspiring to me is to see the lives of the hard-pressed, faith-filled poor," I added. Shaheedul's disappointment was evident. Most Muslims presume the Quran has great attractive power for all who read it. It is good he extracted an admission from me that the Quran (in English translation, not Arabic) does not automatically captivate even the most sympathetic reader.

Shameem, my cheerful nine-year-old neighbor, and his buddy, Polok, stood beside me as I sat outdoors reading. Shameem tried to explain me to Polok: "Uncle Bob is a Christian. He believes Jesus is little Allah." That point was made without sarcasm or disapproval. He was simply stating the matter as he perceived it, or as older Muslims had explained it to him. "No," I explained to the boys, "there is no little Allah. Jesus is the model for my life. As Jesus did, I try to do. Shameem received the correction gracefully. I hoped he would repeat our conversation to whoever misled him about Jesus's role in my life.

After a six months' interval, I visited the parents of Shefali, a girl who died of liver cirrhosis at age twelve despite our efforts. Her mother was particularly glad to

see me again because she had something to get off her chest. "Habibur Leader told us you returned to Shefali's grave after the burial and dug her up. Is it true?" I assured her it is false and that whoever invented such a vicious rumor is no friend of her family. Good works done for needy persons are appreciated by nearly all Muslims and Hindus. A few, however, resent our closeness to the poor and sow suspicion.

As the man came toward me from a distance I understood from his gaze and gait that he intended to intercept me. Straightaway he asked, "How can I join your community?" I quizzed him: "Which community is that? Do you mean the human community?" He waved away my incomprehension. "No, No! I mean your Christian community." "What is your religion?" I asked. "Islam," he stated. "Is Islam not a good religion?" I continued. "Yes, surely, but then how can I go to your country?" he reasoned. Though misguided, at least he was honest.

Torun, one of the seminarians assigned to live with me for a few weeks, is a mature young man—and a good bicyclist. Together we journeyed widely throughout Narail District. In village Narayanpur, within a short distance of each other, we found Sonia, age 10, having an acutely distended abdomen, Farida, 35, bedridden with an undiagnosed illness, and Rima, 7, a severe burns victim (whose burial we attended days later). Torun told me afterward he had never seen persons with such conditions in all his years. He values his exposure to their lives.

Early one morning, before birds chirped or the call to prayer sounded, I overheard a conversation coming through the flimsy wall of the hut closest to mine. He spoke about Allah; she likewise spoke of Allah. Pillow talk about The One. As a topic of conversation Allah comes up habitually among Bangladeshi Muslims. These people remember their Creator. That habit helps make Bangladesh a wholesome place to live.

Devout Muslims Offer Hospitality

October 31, 2009
Narail

The best place in Bangladesh to find men for serious conversation is the tea stall. One day, men at a tea stall in Narail town watched me as I oiled my bicycle. They sent someone to fetch me. Bike in hand, I walked over to join them. They were ten, all involved in trucking. Jahangir put questions to me supplied to him by Kamal and Ratan—the usual questions about my source of income, my wife and children, and my country of birth. When I left them after ten minutes I shook their hands. Jahangir's final comment was about how fortunate they felt to hear the reason for my living among them, that is, the life and teachings of Jesus.

In Bongram, another village, a farmer ran to the road from his rice field shouting for me to stop. Still panting but happy to have caught the "doctor," he informed me of a child in need of surgery, whose address I recorded. Then the farmer asked about my service. I explained briefly I am a Christian missionary. Seconds later, he asked, "You are a Muslim, no?" I repeated and expanded the previous explanation but he failed again to grasp it. For, he reasoned: "If you are a Christian, why would you help Muslims?"

As I rode through Chalito bazaar a roadside tea stall operator called out: "Where have you been? The last time we saw you here was a month ago." I parked the bicycle and sat down to receive tea and questions. Several men, all curious, sat beside me. "Why do you stay in this country? Everyone knows Bangladeshis will do anything to go to your country." I spoke of things I like about their motherland: natural beauty, attractive people, and tasty food. They smiled knowingly. Then, I mentioned the deeper reason for staying: "In Bangladesh I have scope for helping more persons in need than in any other place I know." They became quiet and thoughtful. When I got up to leave I asked where I could rent a cellphone because I wanted to contact a doctor. One of the men whipped out his personal cellphone for my use. It was his way of participating in service to the poor as did his Prophet Isa, that is, my model, Jesus.

Nahar, the sixteen-year-old daughter of Alom, my nearest neighbor, came to my door to announce: "We have a guest. He is a crazy man," she giggled. I asked Nahar whether or not she had seen him before. "Oh, yes," she replied, "He has eaten here before. Abba (Daddy) likes to stand closely when he, or others like him, eat. Abba urges them to eat more. Abba says when you feed a crazy person it makes Allah happy." The irony of it is that Daddy, the enthusiastic feeder of crazies, is materially speaking the poorest man in our neighborhood, but so wise: a devout Muslim who offers hospitality to those who have no way of repaying him.

On the day after the Islamic celebration of Korbani Eid, Nahar came to invite me to a meal that day at 2:30 p.m.. Then she went about preparing a spicy meal. As fuel for their clay stove she started to dismantle the wall of the cooking shed in which she sat tending the stove. It was the only available source of brittle jute sticks. While Nahar was tossing pieces of the wall into the fire to make my meal I experienced a lesson in hospitality.

On Bengali New Year, 1416, Nahar returned home from her short-lived job in the garment industry in Dhaka. As evening approached, her mother, Jahanara, informed me, "Our daughter will be wedded this evening." When darkness fell, a Muslim judge came to Alom's house to record the marriage of Nahar and Babu. A lower-keyed wedding I had never seen. I kept thinking: "What a heartache it must give the girl to be given away so simply." Months before when Jasmeen, a teenaged neighbor, was married, I had noticed the longing in Nahar's eyes for just such an event to make her own wedding wonderful. Jasmeen, an only child, although poor, was afforded a simple banquet, tables and chairs, invitees, music and an amplifier. How disappointed Nahar must be, thought I, that her once-in-a-lifetime celebration had been cancelled due to poverty. But, no, I must hand it to the lady. She was joyfully radiant on her wedding day.

One evening, at 11:00, I returned by bus from having admitted children in Dhaka hospitals. A light rain was falling as I set off on the final walk home in the dark. Minutes later, I felt a bite on the top of my foot, flashed my light, and saw a two-foot-long snake slithering away. "Uh-oh," I thought, "the whole town is asleep by now. What to do but pray for deliverance?" Reaching home, I disturbed Alom's sleep. He listened groggily to my problem and swung into wide-awake action. Over six thousand people die from snake bites yearly in Bangladesh, so villagers treat the problem urgently. He called for Kobad, an exorcist. While awaiting him, Alom prayed aloud in Arabic, massaged my calf, and blew on my foot. Then Kobad prayed to Allah and with his right hand put pressure on me, starting at the top of my head and working down to my foot. No stone was used nor incision made, they simply invoked the Almighty—as did I, but silently. In the morning, Alom came to check on me. "Still living," I assured him. "By the grace of the Almighty," he declared.

At the town library where I go to read a newspaper I asked the librarian, Topu, if there were any English books among the thousands in Bengali. He led me to a dark room and pointed out five short shelves. After squinting at 150 books I chose two, dusted them, and brought them to the desk for checking out. Topu gave me a perplexed look. "We don't have a book-loaning system here," he explained. Others in the reading room were watching to see what would be my reaction as Topu declared apologetically, "All books must be read here." I bit my lip and left the books. Moments later, out of earshot of the crowd, Topu approached me. "For you we'll make an exception. But please don't tell anyone you borrowed a book from this library!" As Bangladeshis say, self-mockingly, "This is Bangladesh."

An educated, idealistic 22-year-old fellow bus passenger, Alameen by name, began our chat by asking about my service in Narail town and surrounding district, which he had long observed, "Are you successful?" I replied, "I am able to do something for the poor, so, I am at peace." He was skeptical, saying, "But I do not see you conversing much with people in the town." I could have explained my preference for going out to folks living far from town, but instead replied, "I don't measure success by how much I converse, but, rather, by my availability to serve disabled persons." After a pause Alameen asked me, "What should I do?" "Just ask yourself," I suggested, "how can I be useful to the poor?" May Alameen also enjoy inner peace.

Muslims Remind Me to Practice My Christian Faith

October 31, 2010
Naogaon

Early every morning, neighbor Mira, a typically pretty, 31-year-old Muslim grandmother, brings home the family bull. The animal is strong and well fed, having been supplied with grass to chew all day long. Mira does more than merely lead the bull home by rope through a nose-ring. Rather, she gathers a handful of tender leaves with which to entice the bull, and then runs home while holding the delicious morsel just before its nose, the bull fast on her heels. If she were to trip she would be trampled. A couple of outsiders passing through observed Mira's dash while barely ahead of the bull. "What nerve!" "How daring!" they exclaimed with admiration. Sometimes it takes outsiders to notice and to remind us how extraordinary our neighbors are.

While bicycling through Adompur's bazaar on a narrow highway I swerved to avoid hitting an old man and, instead, smashed into an eight-year-old boy. I saw his scrawny leg twist beneath my front wheel and feared I had broken it. The old man and I picked up the startled boy and took him to the bazaar's only medicine shop. No soap, disinfectant, bandage, or salve was available there for Roqibul's abrasions. I rode away filled with wonder (how slight the injury was) and gratitude (the Merciful One had saved me again). An hour later, I brought from town the proper dressings and found Roqibul at home. The boy, his mother, and sisters were happy for the attention, but even more so for peanuts and a chocolate bar it delighted me to award the spared one.

Nashiron, a neighbor girl, informed me one afternoon that I had initiated a spinach garden. "How so?" I asked. "You know the place behind our hut where you throw the stalks after detaching the spinach leaves? Well, the stalks have caught hold and are producing new spinach," she explained. What was tossed out as garbage had returned as healthy food! In a country having, arguably, the richest soil on earth, "Throw a seed out the window and a bush will soon appear." Sometimes we plant a seed without even being aware of it.

Yearly, during January, the rector of the major seminary sends a theology student to accompany me. Besides our frequent jaunts by bicycle to villages, Sobuz was willing to do the shopping and cooking during three weeks, freeing me to do some overdue writing. His stay was advantageous for all who saw him, for Sobuz is a Garo "tribal" Bangladeshi, one of the less than 2 percent of the nation having Tibeto-Burmese facial features, unlike the features of the 98 percent majority Bengalis. So, thanks to the Creator for exposing many people to a non-Bengali Bangladeshi, a tribal man of the Modhupur Forest who is educated, cheerful, outgoing, and an exemplary follower of Jesus.

Fellow missioner and friend Fr. Doug Venne, with whom I worked closely during these past 36 years—2 years in the Philippines and 34 in Bangladesh—died and was buried in Bangladesh just before this year began. Doug had

been a great athlete; he became an outstanding missioner. Several months after his death I visited again his village and house. Villagers described the storm that only fifteen days previously had struck and ravaged the house. The bamboo walls lay destroyed and rotting. I asked what had happened to the foundation of the house. It had been dug up and the earth used to envelop the roots of hundreds of sapling trees which will soon be transplanted throughout the area. Doug's memory will also survive in the trees of the village for years to come.

At mid-year I moved to Naogaon, a district town seven hours by bus from my former hometown, Narail. Actively assisted by Shaheen, a sympathetic community-conscious businessman, I was able to locate a habitable room and begin to get acquainted in the vicinity. Close by my room is a tiny, cluttered store patronized by many of us, where Kalu, its owner, sits. One day, I learned about his priorities. I wanted to buy a wrapped piece of bread, but Kalu was preoccupied reading an Islamic religious tract. He read in a forceful voice to get the full impact of the author's wisdom. Kalu was so absorbed in reading that he paid no attention to me, his prospective customer. Later, I chided him for ignoring a person in order to recite pious phrases. He did not deny his preference for holy reading over customer service, so I pointed out to him it is a matter on which we differ.

In the room next to mine lives Faeen, age two. While his mother sat close by, he seized a small piece of broken cement to throw at me. I hoped she would restrain the happy hurler; she did not. Faeen threw, and I deflected it. Later, he came forth beaming while carrying a kitchen knife and tapped its blade on my bare leg. Mother, inches away, again said nothing. I wondered if she was telling me: "Do not expect me to discipline or speak harshly to my only son. He is my future. When I become a widow, Faeen's two sisters will be unable to assist me. I need to be on his side now and always."

Nowadays, banana-seller Wahab is the one I go to daily when gathering foodstuffs from the bazaar. He gives me a better deal than the others. Wahab has dealt unselfishly with me ever since the day we first conversed, and he learned I try to aid children needing surgery. He has said nothing explicit to inform me I would regularly receive bananas from him at a good price, but that is what has happened. He participates in Allah's work of compassion by assisting a servant of the poor.

In a distant bazaar I took breakfast at a restaurant while Alom, the owner, and his friend sat near the entrance, gabbing and smoking. Minutes earlier they had overheard me explain celibacy to a curious tablemate. On my way out I grimaced at Alom's smoking and quipped: "Better to eat a banana than smoke a cigarette." Grinning, Alom nodded agreement; they really should kick the harmful habit he seemed to concede. His parting words to me were, however, a reprimand and a challenge: "It is better to marry than to be celibate." All of us chuckled. Teasing is a favorite Bengali pastime.

Though it is true people here easily fall into quarrels, it is also true that during the month of fasting, Ramadan, many Muslims make strenuous efforts, quietly, to overlook trespasses and slights. That is noticeable to me because I am so often biking and experiencing recklessness on roads and streets. Patience and generosity are emphasized during Ramadan. I observe those virtues being exercised during barely avoided accidents, averted because of one party's adjustment to accommodate others' careless driving. Some days, even I hold my tongue and ride defensively in response to traffic indiscipline. Is the spirit of Islamic Ramadan rubbing off on me, or do Muslims merely remind me to practice my Christian faith?

We Have Different Beliefs, But We Are One Family

October 31, 2011
Naogaon

Skinny, awkward, six-year-old Bareek was brought to see me by his skinny, worried mother. A doctor had diagnosed the boy's cerebral palsy. I pledged to arrange a two-week-long course of physiotherapy so that the mother could learn to help her son. On that very day, Haroon and I were hauling earth in baskets to lay as a foundation for my new house. Bareek decided to help us. In his family's cooking shed he found a high-sided rice plate. Working alongside the men, Bareek filled his plate repeatedly, carried it fifteen meters in his odd, jerky gait, and emptied it wherever Haroon and I emptied our basketsful. Bareek labored nonstop as long as we did. Neighbors who observed his voluntary efforts thought, pound for pound, Bareek was the most admirable of all the earth haulers.

Another six-year-old—my bicycle—disappeared one morning from where I had parked it, in front of the post office. A positive consequence of my loss was that I began to take more time to meet and converse with people in the town. One whom I searched for was Rotin, who works in the kitchen of the Das Restaurant making sweetmeats. I had been hoping to encounter Rotin for over a month in order to beg his pardon for my unintentionally rude behavior earlier. Rotin the sweetmeat maker readily pardoned me. How refreshing it felt to experience his unhesitating forgiveness.

Bangladeshis observe that I walk fast and tease me about it. Without actually racing I normally outstride the local folk. However, there is one group I give way to, devout Muslims who are some distance from their neighborhood mosque when the call to prayer sounds. They take off, their faces set for the mosque. These boys and men do not even observe whom they overtake, for they are answering Allah's invitation to ritual prayer. One does well not to interfere with that all-important religious duty of the pious.

We were sitting on the cement bench that spans the neighborhood canal when the topic turned, as usual, to religion. Five grown men and a few boys, all Muslims, listened carefully when I claimed to have read a translation of the Quran. "What did you think of it?" asked one. "I was glad I had read it," I replied, "because it helps me understand your Islamic faith better." Another put a question to me they all had in their minds: "Was your heart moved by the Quran?" As tactfully as possible I answered, "The Book did not stir me." Silence descended on us. "However," I continued, "that is to be expected. For I am a Christian, and the Bible nourishes my spirit. You are Muslims; the Quran nourishes you. We have different beliefs, but we are one family. We all belong to Allah." Accepted.

Every year a seminarian is with me during one month. Hilarius and I bicycled together to distant villages searching for children in need of hospitalization. As we explained our intention to be of use to poor children in need of surgery, a villager declared to Hilarius with astonishment: "I did not know there are people like you!" Hilarius was impressed to glimpse how positively Muslims respond to compassion shown to their needy ones by Christians. Those Muslims, by their tolerance for our religion and appreciation for persons who live merciful lives, enable us to evangelize by our love for the poor.

Curious 25-year-old Dulal conversed with me as we stood at the rice dealer's store. "You mean to say you are keeping the Islamic thirty-days' fast?" he queried, clearly amazed. "Yes," I replied, "for fasting is a good practice." "But you are a Christian, so why fast with Muslims?" he pressed. I responded: "I do it in solidarity with Muslims, especially from sympathy for the hungry. It is something we can do together to bring us all closer to Allah and to one another." Dulal nodded and went his way. I suspect he is mulling it over.

For drinking and cooking water I depend on my neighbors' generosity to share use of their tube well pump.

Once a day I draw sixteen liters to use during 24 hours. One day, while women and girls were using the pump for bathing, I needed water for cooking. Khaleda, a woman having leadership qualities who lives near the water pump, seized my bucket, disappeared behind the curtain that shields the pump and the bathers, and returned to me with the brim-filled bucket. It is no little thing for a Muslim woman to give a helping hand to a nonrelated male. The fact that I am twice her age does not mitigate the danger to her reputation she may face by assisting me. But it is a risk Khaleda was willing to take. May Allah continue to give her courage.

Sitting inside my house and looking out the door I noticed Arjina walking around with a baby in her arms. Suddenly, she tossed the baby inches into the air and caught her, laughing all the while. After she did it a second time I signaled the seven-year-old child to come see me. She came quickly, hugging the baby closely. "Arjina, you should not toss the baby like that. The baby's bones are soft and might break," I counseled. Arjina retorted with scorn for my ignorance, "It's alright! She's my sister!" A big sister's viewpoint.

Several years ago, I lived in another town where there were no Catholics, but I did get to know a solitary Christian named Popy, a tall, likeable, lonely, thirty-ish fellow who lived with his widowed mother and watched lots of television. He was not married then. Recently, I visited that old hometown. As Popy and I sipped tea together he told me he had married. I congratulated him. Then, earnestly and directly, Popy informed me; "I converted to Islam and married a Muslim lady." I urged him to say more, so he

continued: "I only converted for the sake of marriage. I still believe as before." Now he has a new, Arabic name: Hasan. Popy, his nickname, has not changed. Nor, according to him, has his faith. I pray for my divided friend.

At a government hospital fifty kilometers from the town I met Rupa, a Christian nurse. Rupa is a fine example of a Christian living completely surrounded by Muslims and Hindus, performing her professional duties competently and contentedly. Although she would prefer to live among her own faith community, she does not feel orphaned by the church merely because no other Christians live near the place she is assigned by the government. She seems to realize she is Christ's outreach in that remote location. She blooms where she is planted.

The Best Things in Life Are Free!

October 31, 2012
Naogaon

As I sat reading in the doorway of my hut a neighbor carried Meeteela to see me. I stopped reading in order to elicit a smile from the year-old girl whom everybody likes to tote around. Instead of smiling, however, Meeteela pulled back from me. This is not like her, thought I. Her guardian informed me about Meeteela's fear: "The spectacles you are wearing scare her." (In this neighborhood I alone wear eyeglasses.) I removed the specs from my face, and the cap from my head, besides. The accessories having been removed, she rewarded me with a smile of her own. The best things in life are free.

Outside the town's post office, on a chilly morning, two teenaged girls wearing face and body length veils stepped into my path. Even though it is a public place they had the daring to initiate a conversation. Their religious guides caution girls not to behave so boldly. But these are Bengali Muslims, spontaneously sociable. The lasses' faces were mostly covered, but laughing eyes revealed they were delighted by our meeting. They told me they had once seen me bicycling in their far-distant village. They simply wanted me to know they recognized me.

Kookee, a disabled, middle-aged woman who begs door to door to support herself and her mother, was newly returned from making her daily rounds. She sat in the corner tea stall of our bazaar counting the coins people had given her. Counting was difficult; her eyes are bad. Finally, she finished. Her day's income amounted to 16 takas (20 cents U.S.). Then, Kookee treated herself to a cup of tea—poured into a saucer to make it easier to soak a small piece of hardened bread. It was both her breakfast and a reward for successful Friday morning begging. Her livelihood depends on one of the five pillars of Islam: almsgiving.

In village Shingbasha a wind and rainstorm struck with force, prompting me to knock urgently on a farmer's door to request shelter for myself and bicycle. The storm passed in thirty minutes, so I resumed my journey. Minutes later, on another path, a farmer frantically signaled me to avoid a power line brought low by the storm. I swerved in the nick of time. The elated look on my benefactor's face expressed what he did not say: "The reason I am so happy is I just did something gallant. I saved you."

We were seated in our assigned seats on the fast-moving Ekota Express train when it made an unscheduled stop to take on military personnel. The entire seventy-seat railcar was swiftly evacuated to make space for the soldiers, except for the four of us: Ashraf, age six, released that day from a hospital, his grandmother, uncle, and me. Though a soldier browbeat me to leave, I declined, and beseeched my companions to stay put. Later on, the officer in charge of the soldiers invited me to sit with him. Major Naim, a former U.N. peacekeeper in Sudan, was born in 1976. I came to Bangladesh in 1975. Bengalis respect age, and I had seniority.

While visiting the home of Ain Uddin he complained to me of weakness. Ain is diabetic, so I urged him to do the

exercises that will help control his condition. "I do exercise!" Ain protested. I know the man not to be the energetic type and was skeptical of his claim. "What exercises do you do?" I inquired. "I do my prayers five times daily!" Ritual prayer requires standing, bowing, prostrating, and sitting on one's legs and ankles. It is exercise, true, but may be not the kind needed to impede diabetes.

One afternoon, friendly store-owner Probir greeted me warmly and clarified for me the reason for the long red paste mark down the center of his forehead. He spoke of Krishna and that Hindu god's relevance for his life. We both rejoice in the freedom we share to speak of what and who is meaningful to us. Probir was not preaching to me. He was felicitating me, sharing with me the encouragement he feels from his faith. Won't it be splendid when we all—Muslims, Hindus, Christians, all—can speak and listen to others explain what inspires us without quarreling about it?

Shaheen had recently returned from a month away in Saudi Arabia, on pilgrimage. "How was the experience?" I asked. Shaheen spoke of the hundreds of thousands of Muslims gathered in one place, of the heat at noonday when pilgrims left their air-conditioned rooms to go for prayer, and of eating camel's meat. "Are you glad you went?" I asked. "Definitely!" my businessman friend exclaimed. "Did you make any resolutions there, such as to read the Quran more regularly?" I queried. "No," he easily admitted, for the pilgrimage is not a retreat but, rather, a duty. Having fulfilled that duty Shaheen feels spiritual security.

Early in the morning I bicycled to Chawk Darap village through intermittent rainfall. There, I stopped to notify Sumi, and Tara, her aunt, of our impending trip to the hospital. At their broken-down, mud-walled home Sumi and her family came out to meet me. They were embarrassed not to have any food to offer me—especially because it was the week of their grandest Islamic festival, Eid-ul-Fitr. Eid is a time for heightened hospitality, which, in Bangladesh, always involves food. Their inability to place a snack in front of me assures me how favored I am by God to be able to serve truly needy families. Indeed, the best things in life are free!

Christian Living,
the Witness of Practical Love

October 31, 2013
Hobiganj

During a visit to one of the ten towns I have lived in Bangladesh I was walking on a side street when the face of a young man coming toward me lit up with astonishment. "Do you know who I am?" he asked. I did not. "I am Razzak," he said before adding with a big smile, "The Queen's boy!" Then I remembered! Razzak had been a perilously emaciated child whom I took, along with his mother, to the Children's Nutrition Unit in Dhaka in the mid-'80s, There, Razzak recovered and blossomed. When a member of the English royal family visited Dhaka she paid special attention to the shriveled boy. Afterward, the staff dubbed Razzak "the Queen's boy." He is a fine-looking clerk in a shop. I do not know which one of us was more delighted by our chance encounter. Ordinarily, I never again see the children I have been privileged to help.

At the beginning of the year a seminarian spent some weeks with me. One morning, Kevin and I bicycled to a distant village intending to arrange with parents for the hospitalization of their child. However, the child was no longer there. His father had vacated their village home and taken the family elsewhere in search of work. The child's need for professional treatment was dwarfed by the family's need for food. First things first. Meanwhile,

151

Kevin and I continued to try to be useful to the poor, sometimes successfully.

Months earlier, Bishop Bejoy had sent me an invitation: "Come spend some years in my diocese." Eight months later, we met to iron out the details. Thus, at the beginning of May, I, with no little assistance from the Lord, inserted myself in Hobiganj District of Sylhet Diocese. Bishop Bejoy appreciates this missionary approach to Muslims and Hindus. "First comes the witness of Christian living, the witness of practical love," he affirms with enthusiasm.

During my first days in Hobiganj town I walked and talked, that is, walked up and down the mile-long main street and spoke with all who looked like they wanted to converse. At a bookstore, a lady teacher, hearing of my need to find a room, suggested I see the headmaster of the government high school just across the street. Headmaster Gaffar was sympathetic and offered me a teacher's room on campus for "up to four months' duration." Through Gaffar, God was clearly intervening in my quest for shelter in the crowded town.

In village Tetuia, Tanvir's grandfather, Rajob Ali, was so happy to receive his seven-month-old grandson home after surgery that he wanted to reward me. Rajob offered me fresh milk and went through the motions of milking the family's cow to make it clear to me the milk would be unadulterated. However, not even his pantomime convinced me to accept warm milk fresh from the udder, especially because many cows in Bangladesh suffer from tuberculosis or worm infestation. I thanked him for the kind offer and explained why I stopped drinking milk age eighteen: because my bones were already strong by then.

During Ramadan, the Islamic month of fasting, Mamoon invited me into his home. When he and his wife started to prepare a snack for me I reminded him that I, also, was keeping the fast with them. His mouth fell open in surprise. "You are a Christian and you are fasting with us?" Mamoon threw his arms around me. "You are doing so much for us!" Mamoon credited me with doing good for all Muslims by keeping the fast with them. Solidarity.

Hamid, the wiry, retired gateman of the high school, always asks me whether or not I have eaten. That is the normal way for Bengalis to show regard for their partners in conversation. I had just eaten supper, so I itemized for Hamid what I had eaten: rice, vegetable curry, lentil soup, and cucumber. He smiled upon hearing the familiar names: "We eat, we live, we die, all according to the time Allah has fixed for us," Hamid commented. He knows there is more to life than eating. Even so, he enjoys hearing precisely what I ate—even if they are always the same four items.

As I crossed a bridge to catch a bus, Parul, an NGO officer, was also crossing, on the way to her village office. She is a quite pretty woman and wears an Islamic veil that leaves her face uncovered. Thus, people can see it and praise the Creator. "What is his relationship to you?" the conductor of our bus asked Parul when she paid both our fares. "He is my grandfather," she smiled back. Friends have told me how cool it is to have grandchildren. I know the feeling.

When I prepared to bicycle away from the library, a collegian was waiting for me on the path. "I wish to converse with you," he began. "I like what you do. I also would like to serve the people." Not much more was said. Urging him to continue focusing on ways by which he could be even more useful to others, I called on the Best Giver to bless the young man.

Several times I had purchased bananas at Nozrul Islam's fruit stand, but our first conversation came later. He knew no other Christians. It pleased him to learn I wish to help unite people. "There are many similarities between Muslims and Christians," he proposed. I agreed with his insight and added that I believe there are deep similarities between persons of all faiths. Nozrul nodded his assent seriously but said no more. He may have been accustomed to dwelling on the dissimilarities between himself and persons of other faiths. The truth is we are all one family.

The Poor Commiserate with the Poor

October 31, 2014
Hobiganj

"I have no money" was always Shuhel's excuse for refusing my offer to take him, his wife Parveen, and disabled son Akash to the physiotherapy center. Even though I had pledged to pay their way and other expenses, he felt he must take along some money as insurance against the unknown. Finally, he scraped up a small amount and we departed. When we reached the city after four hours of travel, a blind man got on our bus and announced his need for alms from tenderhearted passengers. I saw only one donor respond: Parveen. She handed a sizeable offering to Shuhel to place in the blind man's hand. The poor commiserate with the poor.

My closest neighbors, Kamrul and Jasna, have six children, ages one to thirteen years. Nitu is six years old and eager to start school. The school's administrator is putting her off because she cannot believe the little girl is age six. For Nitu is not only small; she is also bald and hairless. She has progeria, that is, premature aging, and appears to be a little old woman. Meanwhile, as Nitu waits for permission to enter school, she practices the alphabet and behaves as a pupil under her mother's compassionate tutelage.

155

Sumon, Mitu, and Mahe, three high schoolers, stopped me outside Mamoon's store. They were curious to hear about my life and labors. After a few questions and attentive listening to my replies, Sumon spoke of having seen me bicycling around and hearing about the service I offer to disabled children. "We hope to do that someday," he declared for the trio. "If you do," I predicted, "yours will be happy lives."

A long, muddy ride resulted mostly in exercise one morning. Azizul, whom I intended to see at his home, was beyond reach. His neighborhood was flooded. No boat was available, and I could not shout loud enough to be heard by him. There was nothing to do but return to my base. However, the time was not wasted. Other villagers learned my purpose for coming and understood my desire to help Azizul's child. That purpose remained unfulfilled. But there is no such thing as wasted time in mission, for people are always observing us, scrutinizing us. It is good for them to see our disappointment when we are unable to help one of them.

On the fifth day of the month of Ramadan I was biking to the bazaar on the main street of Hobiganj. A youthful bicyclist, carrying behind him a larger lad, lost control and steered into me. Skin on the back of my hand ripped. Because it was the month of Islamic fasting and Muslims do strive to bridle their tempers and quarrelsomeness, both youths remained calm and conciliatory. The larger boy even fetched an old newspaper to blot my bleeding hand. I, however, was stern and not inclined to act the affably wounded one. In that, I missed out on a purpose for fasting in Islam: to make us more tolerant and forgiving.

One later afternoon, a vivacious, betel nut-chewing Muslim woman stepped into my room as I was reading and addressed me in the local dialect. (The Bengali language has local variants.) Her speech was made even more garbled by the wad of betel nut and leaves in her mouth. I smiled while she spoke. What else is there to do when you see someone is trying to please you? After a few minutes, she departed. Soon afterward, Kamrul and Jasna teased me. "Did you understand what she said to you?" I admitted, "I got that she is a widow, but not much else." The couple laughed and informed me: "She suggested your union with her in marriage!" Such neighborliness I have rarely found in Bangladesh.

Every January and part of February I am accompanied by major seminarians, one at a time for two or three weeks each. This year, Nicholas, James, and I did together the things I am accustomed to doing alone during the other eleven months: bicycling, searching for disabled children, food shopping, cooking, praying. I do not claim our community of three created any special environment in our locality. Nor were all our encounters with Muslims and Hindus sweet. Nevertheless, we did have ample opportunities to witness our faith in the midst of a multitude who are, willy-nilly, witnesses of their faiths to us. January is always a good month for mission and for building harmony.

On a brief return to Tangail, the district where I lived thirty years earlier, I borrowed a bicycle in order to visit villages and old friends. There I met Shaju's wife and children, a happy family. In 1980, Shaju was four years old, had kwashiorkor and weighed twelve pounds. We took him to a hospital just in time. He grew healthy; Allah is merciful. Shaju's four-year-old daughter has an intriguing name: Ma Morium, that is, Mother Mary. Do Muslims respect Jesus's mother? Indeed they do.

During April, Headmaster Gaffar invited me to the high school's Beginning of Spring celebration. Songs were rendered for three hours for the largely middle-class parents of the institution's students. Gaffar requested me to say something to the gathering. I ended my remarks saying, "Service is the best religion," which caused them to break into applause. The folks seem to understand this Christian missionary is among them to serve the poorest and neediest in their bodily needs, and for no other hidden agenda.

There is a statement of the church's teaching from the document entitled *The Relationship of the Church to Non-Christian Religions* that I have almost memorized. "Let Christians, while witnessing to their own faith and way of life, acknowledge, preserve and encourage the spiritual and moral good found among non-Christians, as well as the values in their society and culture." To the One Who prompts all of us to acknowledge, preserve, and encourage that which is admirable and good among non-Christians all thanks be given.

To Other Towns, Therefore, I Must Go

October 31, 2015
Hobiganj

"The peace of Allah be upon you, my brother!" was shouted at me by a passenger in a noisy motorized rickshaw as it passed me. Whenever I bicycle outside Hobiganj town men acknowledge me. It was not so thirty months ago, when I first arrived in this district. Then there was suspicion, for I claimed to be a Christian missionary. Such persons are presumed to work solely for Muslims' conversion from Islam to Christianity. As months passed and more parents with their children accompanied me to hospitals for treatment, trust grew. Now that I intend to spend only another half year among them there is affection for the missionary. Indeed, the peace of Allah is upon me!

There are many more persons here whom I could help, so why should I move to another town and district? I simply wish to continue making signs of brotherhood to Muslims and Hindus, just as I have done in the previous eleven towns and districts. The life of service to the sick-poor and simplicity of lifestyle say to those among whom I dwell, "We are one human family." Besides that, if I were to remain beyond three years some persons whose suspicions of my motives never ceased will have reason to suspect I am merely biding my time and will eventually attempt to entice Muslims to abandon Islam for Christianity. To other towns, therefore, I must go.

Has this approach to mission accomplished anything? A lot of children have been helped, that is, kids having cerebral palsy, burn contractures, cleft lips and palates, and more. Meanwhile, I have received collaborators and edifiers.

Early Monday mornings I meet Mamoon at the Taj Restaurant for hot bread and lentils. It is my way of showing appreciation for Mamoon's on-going involvement in works of mercy. By cellphone he helps me communicate with villagers who wish to see me. Sometimes, villagers speak so excitedly I cannot understand them. Mamoon intervenes to get the information I need. Recently, he purchased a used bicycle so he, too, can enjoy good health. Last Christmas Day, he was delighted to be with me at the jail, where I was privileged to shake hands with eight hundred prisoners while giving them each an orange. Mamoon is not my follower. We are brothers in service to the poor, Muslim and Christian collaborators.

In muddy Kashipur I needed to make a telephone call. Having no cellphone of my own I requested the use of Jahangir's phone as we sat together in the village tea stall. Quickly, he agreed, for he knew I had come to his remote village for the purpose of aiding disabled, deformed, and diseased children. Jahangir was deeply pleased to cooperate in a work of mercy, for the Merciful One blesses the merciful.

A motorcyclist named Mukit overtook me on the street and told me he wished to speak with me. He recommended a disabled child to me. Standing beside my bicycle I wrote the child's name and address on a slip of paper—my customary messy file of persons to be seen.

"When will you visit the child?" Mukit asked me. "Allah alone knows," I replied, "but it will be soon, God willing." Men and women, even complete strangers, feel blessed when they guide my steps to persons in need.

Shuab's only son needed surgery. His wife was not in favor of accompanying me, but Shuab prevailed. Together we traveled five hours by bus to Dhaka, where the child was operated on successfully. Since then, the slight, energetic peddler of fresh cows' milk has introduced me to others whose children need treatment. Shuab allays parents' distrust of me and quietly assures them that my

161

purpose pleases Allah. He and I do the same thing: share what the Creator gives us with the poor.

At a meeting of priests I was asked: "What is the reaction of Muslims to your work and your presence among them?" I mentioned only one fact. A significant number of high school and college youth wish to speak with me. Some state frankly, "I want to do what you are doing." I urge them to retain their insight into the happiness our service yields. They have no problem perceiving that the good works and the lifestyle they see are because Jesus is my model in life.

Before she reached one and one-half years of age Niha was already being catechized by her mother, Jasna. Niha repeated the words as well as she could. Her three older brothers, especially Rayhan, age fourteen, supplemented Mother's lessons. Rayhan patiently but firmly demanded Niha's correct pronunciation of every word of the expression "There is no god but God." Within a few months that central teaching of Islam will be ineradicably a part of Niha. This is catechizing at its best: learning from one's own family to remember the Creator.

Acquaintances from Dhaka came to visit me. I had assured Jasna, mother of the family from whom I rent a room, that it would not be necessary for her to offer them a snack. Nevertheless, she spread a tablecloth and laid on it biscuits, cakes, bananas, a spicy mix, and mango juice. After the guests had gone I tried to convince Jasna to accept some money to defray her expenses. Cheerfully but resolutely she pushed away my money-bearing hand, saying: "I did it because hospitality is my religion." I can believe it.

I Seek Collaborators

October 31, 2016
Shariatpur

"Thank you," or its Bengali language equivalent, is not spoken often in the twelve towns I have lived in in Bangladesh. Consequently I marveled at my youngest neighbor, Niha, age three years, when she started telling me—in English and for no apparent reason—"Thank you very much." This is she who loves to be outdoors during heavy rains, where she runs and shouts and collapses merrily in the mud. Yet, Niha has already mastered the use of one of the most gracious expressions in the English language: "Thank you very much."

Three teenaged boys stopped me near the town's stadium. "We want to interview you for our high school's annual magazine." By the time their questions and my answers ended another seven boys had joined us, listening respectfully. They are attracted to service for the poor, which they see wins respect for the server. They already intuit there is more to life than earning money.

In a large distant village to which I bicycled every first Tuesday, Moin Uddin, a government health worker, had become my collaborator. While a group of men sat in a tea stall near the hospital, Moin regaled us by flawlessly speed-reading a newspaper article as articulately as a rapper. He made us howl! Many persons of the place regard Moin as eccentric. My regard for him is full of respect and affection. For I seek collaborators, and Moin is one of them.

Early one chilly morning, I arrived at the home of Jahangir, his wife, and son. It was my third visit to see them. This time, we set the date for taking his son to Dhaka for surgery. As I was leaving their home, Jahangir ran after me to ask something that made him deeply curious. "Brother, what is your religion?" My reply: "Christian," at which he sighed flatly, "Oh." Like many other Muslims, Jahangir wishes I were one of them. It would make him feel better to be helped by a fellow Muslim.

Borhan manages a three-wheeler cab service. When he sees me pass by on bicycle he invites me to take tea with him. "I like you very much!" he has often told me. Eagerly he informs others about my efforts for disabled children. Borhan's rare ambition is to someday be able to build an animal hospital to shelter the many stray dogs of the place, one of which lay peacefully at his feet as we sipped our tea together.

When my three years' stay in Hobiganj neared its end Bishop Bejoy wished for me to move to another one of the four districts in his Sylhet Diocese. However, I was intent on moving far away, and he understood my missionary purpose. Accordingly, he arranged a farewell meal for me, at which gifts were given and his blessing bestowed on my future in the Barisal Diocese.

Around the time I was switching dioceses assassinations and executions were occurring throughout the country with greater frequency than ever. Thus, when I visited one of my former hometowns, Ataur, the dwarf, who is doorman at the Chinese restaurant, was delighted to see me once more. Ataur led me by the hand through the bazaar while announcing "Bob Brother is alive!" Many people had heard the news that a Christian missionary had been shot, and, as they know only one foreign missionary they imagined I had been the victim.

In my new hometown, Shariatpur, I had hoped to be able quickly to attract parents by my offer of treatment for their disabled children. Within two weeks I had won over Kulsuma and Malek to accompany me with their child, Alameen, to Dhaka. On the day before our departure I returned to reassure them about our trip. Kulsuma, the boy's mother, requested me to sit down. She had a hard time saying what she had to tell me. "You are a foreigner," she began. What she meant was: "We are suspicious of you. No one has ever offered to help us as you do. We fear trickery. We cannot go with you." Thus did I understand that I am once again starting from scratch in a new mission area.

During my first visit to Noria's large bazaar I took breakfast in a dark restaurant. Another customer, without any preliminary comments, leaned over and inquired, "Your age is one hundred plus, no?" To which I replied, "My looks have deceived you." There are few one-hundred-year olds in Bangladesh, and perhaps not one of them pedals a bike ten miles to get breakfast.

The police feel inconvenienced by my presence in Shariatpur, the only foreigner in their district. Assassinations occasionally occur throughout the country. It is their job to maintain security for all, especially for foreigners. Several officers have told me: "You cannot live among the poor, because there you are easily exposed to harm. You must live within a walled compound. Do not venture out of doors; stay inside. Go abroad for a long vacation." All their warnings are well meant. They are uneasy about the foreigner's safety. I appreciate their concern, and on my daily bicycle journeys frequently recall one officer's advice: "Keep looking over your shoulder." That much I can do.

We All Serve That One

October 31, 2017
Shariatpur

A bulldozer was busy recently along the main street through Shariatpur town destroying businesses that had been built illegally on the side of the road. An eatery, a repair shop, a tea stall, all constructed of lumber or tin came crashing down, their owners standing nearly in order to salvage the remains. The owners knew this day would come. So, why did they not take action earlier to avoid the ruination? Were they hoping for a reprieve permitting them to stay? Or, perhaps, they simply knew of no other place to relocate. Space is scarce in Bangladesh.

"May I ask you a question?" a teenager asked me. "Surely," I said. "What is your religion ... Islam?" My single word reply: "Christian." "Oh," he responded soberly, and then retreated. Numerous persons here during my now-concluded first year in their town liked what I proposed to do with them but not what I am. Why, they wondered, would a Christian be so concerned for disabled Muslims? At many a tea stall the aged foreign bicyclist was a topic of conversation and scrutiny.

One morning in Mohammadpur Bazar youths described to me another youth suffering from "paralysis." I saw no need to go look at the fellow, for what could I possibly do for a twenty year old stricken with polio. Nevertheless his chums cajoled me, so I went and found Sumon with several maladies. We arranged for the ailing youth to travel via bicycle van to the town's hospital. I am glad I went to see Sumon, for his friends' diagnosis had been mistaken. Usually it is a good idea to accompany folks when they persist in requesting it. Trust grows that way.

Kids here are wild about cricket. There was no school in session one day as I bicycled through Kachari village where boys were playing the game on the school grounds. I heard the smack of a ball on bat. Quickly thereafter a red ball appeared rolling down the road directly in front of me. Good hit, I thought, and if it keeps rolling they will have to fish the ball out of the drainage ditch beside the road. Accelerating, I caught up with the ball and halted it with one foot. Boys on both teams cheered the rescue.

A motorcycle-for-hire driver practicing his English on me asked, "Your hour?" His question puzzled me because I saw he was wearing a wristwatch. So, I checked my pocket watch and told him, "7:07." He rubbed his chin in confusion as if to say, "How can I make this foreigner understand?" From nearby a fellow driver spoke up. "He wants to know your age." For clarification I asked, "In years or in hours? If he wants my age in hours (here I took some moments to calculate), slightly over 700,000 hours is my age." Now he can practice his arithmetic, too.

Junayed, an eighteen-month-old boy, is the only child of poor parents in a faraway village where I try to be useful. Twice I have been at hospitals with him and Lovely, his mother. Finally, a kind doctor told his mother frankly that her son will always have Down Syndrome and she should expect little help from medicine. When I had first seen Junayed I realized he had DS, so why make the effort to help him? Because everyone's life counts. Even though Junayed may never "earn his keep" or help his community he deserves as much as can be provided by medical professionals and neighbors. Besides, Junayed does indeed enrich the community. Everyone loves the little guy.

Tea stall operator Hatem, in Chandropur Bazar, always seems pleased when I drop in. In that area of the district I have not yet been able to help many children, but he knows my purpose is to assist the disabled and seriously infirm children, and he wishes to have a part in that. Hatem does not charge me for the tea I drink. Always I offer him payment, and he pleasantly refuses it. "We all serve that One," he proclaims, while urging me to return soon for "tea on the house."

One night, all night long, loudly amplified sermons and singsong praises of Allah were broadcast from the nearby mosque. Next day a preacher glorified the most important duty of Muslims, the offering of Islamic ritual prayer. Often when I converse with Muslim men I ask them what is the purpose of our lives. If they were to answer according to what their preachers emphasize they might readily say, "Faithfulness to ritual prayer." When I propose love for others as the foremost purpose of our lives they often nod thoughtfully in agreement. But they have been taught that ritual prayer is their highest religious obligation.

Ali Ahmed, an energetic seventy-year-old advocate, prides himself on being an honest lawyer. "The people love me," he declares. During the second largest of the Islamic festivals, Korbani Eid, he fed me at his home. After community prayers Muslims stay at home on this feast day preparing and enjoying food—but also sharing their freshly slaughtered meat. As soon as he had fed me, his guest, Ali was off to distribute meat among the poor in his neighborhood. I always enjoy visiting Ali in his office where he is surrounded by images of his favorites, Mahatma Gandhi, Karl Marx, and Mother Teresa.

After a morning bicycle trip I returned to town and sat reading the daily newspaper in the public library. Someone approached me. I lowered the newspaper and found before me an unknown, smiling, thirteen-year-old lass with hand extended toward me. In her hand was a wee chocolate candy bar. Though much surprised I accepted her gift. Not a word was uttered—the girls keep library rules better than the boys—as she withdrew silently. Even without words she made a Christian missioner feel welcomed, trusted, and even liked.

Postscript

Father Bob McCahill originally suggested a different title for this little book of letters: "Better than No Uncle." He quoted a Bengali saying: "A one-eyed uncle is better than no uncle at all." That saying is a variation on another saying: "Something is better than nothing." As I compiled his annual letters into this book he wrote: "In my life of involvement with the sick and disabled poor it is my intention to bring physical improvement to all the young people I can. If they are below age fifteen years, poor, and have serious health problems I may be able to help them. Maybe. No guarantees are given. Anyway, I shall try to be helpful, useful to them. Perhaps I shall fail, but at least they will know someone tried to do the needful in their time of difficulty. My attempt to help is better than would be its neglect or absence. It is better for them to have a commiserater than no one at all. It is better to show compassion to persons than to declare their cases hopeless."

Victor Edwin, SJ
Director of the Vidyajyoti Institute
of Islamic Studies in Delhi, India